I0414792

WHAT IT TAKES

THINGS A CANADIAN POLICE OFFICER WANTS YOU TO KNOW ABOUT HIS JOB

Owen R.B. Roberts

 FriesenPress

One Printers Way
Altona, MB R0G 0B0
Canada

www.friesenpress.com

Copyright © 2023 by Owen R. B. Roberts
First Edition — 2023

All rights reserved.

No part of this publication may be reproduced in any form, or by any means, electronic or mechanical, including photocopying, recording, or any information browsing, storage, or retrieval system, without permission in writing from FriesenPress.

ISBN
978-1-03-916499-4 (Hardcover)
978-1-03-916498-7 (Paperback)
978-1-03-916500-7 (eBook)

1. POLITICAL SCIENCE, COMMENTARY & OPINION

Distributed to the trade by The Ingram Book Company

DEDICATION

To those who stay up all night.

To those who sit with their backs to the wall.

To those who take their seatbelts off
as they round the last corner.

To those who wear the uniform and exemplify
all the good things described in this book.

To my brothers and sisters across this country
who work hard to hold the line.

(And to those who wake up at night,
praying for their safety.)

Do your job well and hold your head high.

TABLE OF CONTENTS

INTRODUCTION

POLICE OFFICERS ARE TASKED WITH protecting life and property. In the real world this translates into fulfilling many roles: taxi driver, babysitter, counsellor, teacher, social worker, and infantry soldier. Police officers must be expert listeners and communicators, they must know the law and they should be in good physical condition so they can run a mile at a second's notice. They must make decisions—important decisions that come with consequences—and they must make them quickly, sometimes in less than a second. To make matters worse, the public expects a quality of performance that approaches perfection, for few people are faulted more quickly for making a poor decision than a police officer.

I have been honoured to serve as a police officer for more than a decade. I have spent most of that time patrolling the streets of a Canadian city significant enough in size to experience every kind of crime and social problem. I have seen the best and the worst of what people have to offer to the world. I have seen my fellow officers work hard and make sacrifices to do their job well and to keep each other and the people of our city safe. I have also seen the dark side of humanity, the stuff that many people do not realize is there. I have seen things that some do not believe can be true and that no one can fully understand unless they have seen it with their own eyes, heard it with their own ears, and smelled it with their own noses.

Through it all I have seen how little people understand of the day-to-day realities of policing in Canada. Even though the entertainment industry has produced myriad policing-related material—some based on true events and some entirely fictional—a great degree of confusion still surrounds police work. The general public simply does not know what it is like to work in the profession. And the average person cannot be blamed for not knowing; there are some good reasons for this.

Police need to keep secrets. In fact, when we are hired, we swear an oath promising not to share certain details with people outside of law enforcement. We are expected to keep quiet about the private details of the lives of people we meet. We cannot talk about ongoing investigations because the people being investigated can destroy evidence or avoid arrest. We cannot share details of how we work through dangerous situations because a successful outcome and our own safety depend upon being able to keep others guessing. In many cases, the law requires that we keep information to ourselves.

However, I feel our tendency to keep secrets may actually be to our own detriment. People criticize police for things that are outside of their control. When bad things happen in our communities people want answers fast and the answers are usually provided slowly, if at all. People often think the worst of police officers and make unfair assumptions about their conduct or motivations. Often we stay quiet in the face of unfair criticism, as if there is no room in the conversation for the facts.

My motive in writing about my profession came from a desire to reduce some of the misunderstanding. I believe this benefits everyone because it is often a misunderstanding that causes a lot of unnecessary hurt and anger.

When I was being trained as a police officer, I was given the following metaphor. Ninety-eight percent of people are sheep. One percent of people are wolves. The remaining one percent are sheepdogs. We, the police, are the sheepdogs. Most people (for argument's sake, about ninety-eight percent of them) are decent people who mean no harm to those around them and want to live as contributing members of society. Like sheep, they do not possess sufficient defences when the wolves attack. And, most assuredly, there are wolves nearby, though their true nature is not fully known to all the sheep.

There is a delicate balance in how police represent crime in their jurisdiction. On one hand, we need people to know that we are playing an important role and we require the funding necessary to do our work. For these reasons, we need citizens and politicians to know that crime is a problem. But on the other hand, we want people to feel safe and know that we are working toward that end. People do not need to know the details of the heinous things going on in their city because those things are not really their problem. In fact, there are many people who could not process this information very well. I myself have friends who simply do not want to hear the gritty details. This is one of the reasons I love my job. I consider it an honour to stand between the wolves and the sheep. I am willing and able to deal with the evil so that the sheep do not need to be concerned about it.

But something frightening has happened in North America. Much energy has been spent trying to convince the sheep that the sheepdogs are the dangerous ones. In doing so, many people, some of whom are very intelligent, have said some baffling things that can only be accounted for by a profound lack of understanding about what is going on in their cities. Essays have been written on how to imagine a world without policing. People have cried for funding to be removed from policing so that social workers and addiction counsellors can do their job instead.

I would be among the first to agree that we need more help for people with addictions and mental health struggles. But if you think that an addiction counsellor would want to face the situations I have encountered, you are blissfully ignorant of what it is like to walk into a house where someone is melting down in crisis.

In the following pages, I will walk you through how a police officer responds to this trend of vilifying the police and explain why the idea of defunding the police is, at best, wishful thinking. I will explain the mindset an officer has to develop to work safely in a dangerous job. I will provide examples of the situations officers encounter daily related to mental health, addiction and violence. Out of my own experiences, I will demonstrate how police are misrepresented in media due to assumptions about the job. I will also admit that we know we are not perfect; critics are necessary to keep us at a high level of professionalism. Finally, this book contains an epilogue describing a fictitious but realistic day in the life of a police officer working on the streets. It may benefit some readers to skip to that section in order to find context for the information provided in the rest of this book.

I am writing this because I believe you will benefit from a fuller knowledge of what it takes to become a police officer, what the job really involves, and what it does to the men and women who do the job. I hope that my perspective will help you gain a better understanding of what it is like to police in Canada. The information you find here will apply directly to those who work to keep your community safe. I will describe some of the things that police typically keep to themselves because there seems to be no appropriate context in which to explain them. These are the things we wish everyone, including our own families, knew about our job. These are the things we want people to know before they fill out an application to work with us.

I am fiercely proud of what I do. I work with hundreds of police officers and we join tens of thousands more across this country who do a job you cannot imagine unless you have had the privilege of doing it yourself. I am not asking you to fully understand our job. What I am asking is that you see that you cannot fully understand it. That is, unless you are willing to come and join us.

1. HIRING AND TRAINING

Bang, bang!

I run down the hall and hide behind the couch in the living room, out of breath. I wait, trying to be silent and listening for footsteps coming toward me. Soon I hear someone approaching. They found me. I jump out from behind the couch.

"Bang! Got you!"

AS KIDS, MY FRIENDS AND I loved to play "cops and robbers." We hid from one another, snuck around the house and surprised one another, firing our toy guns. Then we ran in opposite directions to hide and do it all over again. There were few rules and there was no real winner, no real loser. It was just a game.

Before there was ever a police officer there was a kid who wanted to catch bad guys. There was a boy who wanted to grow up to be like his dad, or a young woman who wanted a job that was also an adventure. There was a person who knew that there was right and wrong and wanted to do something with his life that made a difference. He wanted a job that was meaningful.

As a kid I thought it would be fun to be a police officer. I did not know much about the real world yet, and I knew even less about policing. I knew it would not be like playing cops and robbers with my friends, but I was pretty sure it would be an adventure.

Many years went by before I gave serious thought to the possibility of a career in policing. Even as an adult, there was a sense of mystery and adventure about the idea. In some ways, though I had grown up and learned more about the world, I still knew very little about policing. What I did know was that I slept better at night knowing I could dial 911 if I ever woke up to the sound of my basement window being broken. Part of why I wanted to be a police officer was to help provide that peace of mind to others.

By the time I applied to be a police officer I had worked in a job for most of my twenties in a capacity where I interacted constantly with people. In fact, I served a segment of the population that often interacted with police in unfortunate circumstances. I felt I had learned a lot about people. I knew they could lie and manipulate. I knew a little of what life was like for those who came from broken, dysfunctional, or addiction-ridden homes. But I still had a lot to learn. I had only begun to witness the effects of addiction and domestic abuse. I had not really seen what addiction did to families. I had not seen the squalor in which people lived, even in a wealthy country like Canada.

The Application Process

Everyone who wants to become a police officer comes from a family and a home. They are sons, daughters, brothers, aunts, husbands, and mothers. They come with all of their life experience; they come with their cultures, customs, and religions. They are just people, like you. But they are people who have decided to apply for one of the most exciting jobs on earth.

Submitting an application package is a monumental task. One must fill out a host of forms, including notes from doctors, optometrists, and audiologists who can verify that minimum requirements are met in terms of health, eyesight and hearing. They have to provide a list of all their family members and family members of their spouse. If you are interested in the details, you can visit the website of your local police department and peruse the page that refers to the application process. There you will find just how extensive the process is and how much information is being asked of the applicants before they are even considered for employment.

Applicants are also asked many questions about their past conduct as it relates to ethics. They are required to provide information about all the car accidents they have had and traffic tickets they have received. They are asked to disclose shady activity in their past such as the night they drove home tipsy from a party, or the time they cheated on a test in high school. Some of the answers on the application forms contain information that outright eliminate some people from consideration for the job. These people are never even asked to participate in the hiring competition.

As for those who would withhold information, the rest of the hiring process is designed to try to weed out as many of those people as humanly possible. As the process continues, those fortunate enough to proceed will have further opportunity to hash through the details of their life to the point that they will feel terrible about themselves. All this is done for a couple reasons.

First of all, the police service wants to know what sort of person it is hiring. If just anyone were permitted to don a uniform, the authority they receive would be corrupted in no time. In some countries it is easy to get a job as a police officer. A common experience of citizens in those places is that the police are on their side as long as they have bribe money on hand. Such is not the case in Canada. People of that sort are weeded out of the application process because they are unfit for the job.

Second, the police need to hire people who will be honest about their mistakes. The police service knows it is hiring someone with an imperfect past. Everyone who has lived to adulthood in this world has at least a few things in their past that embarrass them. However, the big deal in policing is not that one must be perfect but that one must admit his mistakes. If a person is able to admit to past wrongs, he is more likely to be honest in his work. It is difficult to overstate the importance of this step in the process because while police officers may come from many different backgrounds, one thing they must all have in common is integrity. Without integrity, we diminish the confidence that the public has in our work.

If an applicant is invited to join the competition there are several preliminary tests to be completed. These tests are generally of three types. There are academic tests that rate the common sense or IQ of the applicant. There are physical tests that one must pass to demonstrate a minimum standard of physical fitness. Also, there are psychological tests intended to determine a person's mental and emotional fitness for the work.

Now we must swing back to the conversation about honesty. One way of establishing that an applicant is honest is submitting her to a polygraph test. The person who administers the polygraph test is an officer who has a great deal of interviewing experience.[1] During the polygraph test the applicant must once again go into detail about her past. This is often a long and difficult day as she is asked to divulge her past deeds as they relate to driving infractions, alcohol and drug use, and any form of criminal activity. Once this test is over the polygraphist provides an opinion to the hiring staff regarding how honest the applicant has been thus far in the process. Of course, if there are red flags the applicant will not be invited to participate further.

---

1 In order to become a polygraphist one must complete a twelve-week-long course, the longest single course in Canadian policing. With lots of on-the-job experience, the polygraphist is very good at determining how honest a person is when they answer questions about their past. I have never worked as a polygraphist, but I think of them as Robert DeNiro's character in *Meet the Parents*. Don't even try to lie to them.

In addition to all these steps there are things going on behind the scenes. Police speak with references, friends, coworkers, and family members in order to get a clearer picture of what kind of person they may be hiring. There might be a visit to the applicant's house to get a sense of the stability of his home life and the level of support from his family.

Lastly, an applicant gets to the final interview, often with a panel of several people. This interview is usually based on past behaviour. The interviewee is not asked why she is the sort of person who will take initiative or why she believes she is honest. Rather she is asked to provide concrete examples of times when she took initiative or when she was honest even though it was difficult. Facing police officers across a boardroom table for several hours is stressful. As part of their assessment, the police officers are watching how the applicant deals with that stress.

This process is thorough and it takes a long time. People are often turned away as the competition is intense. This means that most people who want the job will have to go through most or all of these steps more than once. For some, it takes several years between submitting an initial application and being hired as a police officer.

Finally, the fortunate few are given job offers, marking the start of a life-changing adventure. I remember the day I received that phone call. It was the culmination of a long and arduous process, but my adventure was only beginning.

Why the Process?

Police departments are looking to hire the best available candidates for the job. They want people who will work well as members of a team, speak honestly, and think through situations rather than react instinctively. Policing is always changing and officers must be able to adapt to new working conditions. Years ago the police stopped looking only for people who were physically strong and began looking for people who were also emotionally resilient, intelligent, and street savvy.

In addition to this, in larger departments there are various career paths one could take and a wide variety of work within the profession. The hiring staff know that they need to fill many different roles, and for that they need great variety and diversity in their ranks.

As we have said, one significant reason for the lengthy hiring process is that police officers need to be people of strong character who will be honest even when it is not easy. Honesty is one of the pillars on which Canadian policing and the justice system are built. When a witness is called upon to testify in court, his testimony is assigned a certain value based on how honest he seems. The testimony of police officers needs to carry weight because of the role they play in the justice system. Police are the ones who investigate crimes, find people in possession of stolen property, see the injuries on a victim, or chase and tackle the people who jumped out of a stolen car. Police are the ones who lay charges and testify in court to their role in the investigation. Again, one can find examples around the world of justice systems that are full of corruption due to the fact that judges, lawyers, and police officers are willing to say whatever will win them a bribe. We aim for a higher standard in Canada and, although our system can at times prove itself less than perfect, it is not riddled with the corruption that one finds in many other places. For that, we can be thankful.

Training

When I was hired I went through my training with new police officers who ranged in age from their early twenties to early forties. They had been electricians and truck drivers, youth workers, and university students. They were regular people who wanted an exciting new career. We all had a lot to learn and we had to learn fast.

Throughout the course of our training we focused on physical fitness, self-defence, use of force, Canadian law, and firearms. Two other topics that received a lot of attention were cultural sensitivity and mental health.

Regarding mental health, there were two kinds of conversations. First, we learned how mental illness can affect people and what we could expect when we encountered people who suffered from mental illness. The other conversation was about our own mental health. Our future in policing would put us in places we could not yet imagine. Our instructors knew all too well what this had done to those who had gone before us. They wanted to prepare us as well as they could for what was to come. We will return to both of these topics later.

In retrospect, I believe the goal of our training was to change our view of the world so we would see it the way a police officer sees it. A police officer has to look at the world a little differently to give himself the best chance of staying alive while on the job.

Scare Tactics

I remember hearing countless personal stories from our instructors. These were true stories of people who were policing in the very city in which I would soon be working. There were stories of simple situations suddenly turning dangerous. There were stories of seemingly harmless individuals—sometimes children or elderly people—attacking them without warning. There were stories of fights, brawls, and traffic stops turned ugly. There were stories of times when police officers had to fire their weapons at people.

I also remember watching videos as part of our training. These were not cheesy re-enactments. These were videos of real life events in policing, usually taken from dash cameras in police vehicles. Often these videos could be found online. The videos depicted real-life deadly encounters in which police officers were ambushed or attacked in some way. They were videos of someone's very bad day at work. Sometimes they were videos of someone's last day at work, because the police officer did not survive the events recorded in the video.

Many of the videos began with what appeared to be a benign event. But then, without any warning, the scene turned violent and someone was injured or killed. For a sample of what I am describing, you only need to search online videos for "police shootouts" or "police being attacked" to find plenty of material. But if you choose to do so, know that some of what you find there will be graphic.

Sitting in the classroom, wearing a brand-new uniform, it sunk in for me. There are days when police officers do not come home after work. Perhaps an officer gets up one morning expecting to go camping with his family that weekend. Perhaps another hugs her kids after dinner and heads off to a night shift, saying, "See you in the morning" as she walks out the door. But something unthinkable happens and she does not come home in the morning.

To be sure, people may lose their lives while on the job in many different professions. Lots of people have to adhere to standards of safety in order to avoid injury in the workplace. Farmers must exercise caution around machinery. Electricians must be careful to avoid catastrophic electrocutions. However, there is a difference between most professions and that of policing. The difference is that in policing the injury or fatality is often brought about through the conscious act of another individual. Police officers must be aware of any possible source of danger; we must walk into every building and room as though there is someone in that place who may want to hurt us. In my experience, outside of policing, the most common types of work where this is also true are taxi drivers and convenience store employees who are robbed by violent people on a very regular basis. After this happens, it then becomes the task of the police to identify, locate, and arrest those violent people.

This is why we were trained to look at the world differently. We were taught to walk into a room and immediately identify danger. We learned to watch human behaviour carefully so we could identify the cues of someone preparing to attack us. In short, we learned to be wary of other people and vigilant in every situation. Once a person develops this way of watching the world there is no going back. Later on, once working in the community, our experiences only reinforce the importance of looking at the world this way.

The truth is that every person with whom I interact on the job is a potential danger. The videos I watched and the stories I heard during training all highlighted the fact that no one we meet on the job can be trusted completely. Anyone can become a threat to themselves, to the police, or to someone else. For this reason, my guard is always up, and when I am at work I distrust everyone just the same. I do not care about skin colour; I do not care if you drive a Mercedes or a Mazda. If I pull your car over, I consider you a potential threat until I become convinced otherwise. I have been trained to do so because history has shown that the moment I let my guard down I open myself up to the possibility of the unthinkable. And if I do that, I let my family down. Because I also hug my family before I leave for work and tell them I will see them in the morning.

Teamwork

One of the things that draw people to policing is the idea of being part of a team that works together for the common good. This is one of the things that I love most about my job.

It takes teamwork just to get through all the work that needs to be done in a shift. Life on the street is busy and most days it takes all available hands to get through the workload. However, it becomes even more important that we function as a team when things get dangerous.

For this reason a great deal of our training is focused on teamwork. Our instructors told us it may one day make the difference between life and death. The fact that I work in a larger city means that help from my team is usually not far away if something goes wrong. And things sometimes do go wrong. I can think of more than one time when I radioed for support and heard the sirens coming from all directions. I have also been the one who rushes to help my fellow officers when they called for help. These things tie a group of people together in a way that is hard to describe. We have to entrust our safety to one another and that cannot be taken lightly. For this reason, our training focused on making certain we understood that we had to work hard to ensure the safety of *everyone* on the team.

Eventually my time in training came to an end. I had trained for months and not yet seen the inside of a police car. But that first day on the streets was fast approaching and I knew I still had so much to learn.

2. ON THE JOB

I am driving alone in my police car when I hear the dispatcher's voice on the radio. An ambulance is on its way to a house where a middle-aged woman is having trouble breathing. The house is four blocks away from me.

I turn on the siren and speed off to the rescue. Still new at my job, I am excited that I may get the chance to help someone. Perhaps I will do CPR until the ambulance arrives. Perhaps I can be of some help to this poor woman.

I arrive before the ambulance and see that the front door has been left open in anticipation of my arrival. I dash up the sidewalk and into the house. A man sitting at the dining-room table calmly points me toward a bedroom in the corner of the house and says, "She had too much to drink."

In the bedroom, I find the woman lying in bed amid a sea of empty beer cans. It's noon on a Thursday. The woman is breathing. I know this because she is groaning loudly with each breath. She is so drunk that she does not notice me enter the room.

As I am still processing all this, the EMS members stroll calmly into the bedroom behind me.

"Drunk?"

"Yup," I respond.

"All right. We will take a look. Thanks."

I walk out the front door and back to my car.

AFTER MONTHS OF TRAINING IT was finally time to begin doing the work I wanted to do. I had been waiting for a long time to work as a police officer. I was excited to get into the police car and get straight to it. What I quickly learned was that all the theory I received in training had to be relearned in relation to the real world. There was still so much to understand and it felt like I was starting all over. The time in class can only prepare a person to a certain extent. After that the learning has to be practical; it has to be done in real-life situations.

For this reason, new recruits spend time working with experienced officers. This arrangement usually lasts somewhere between three and six months, depending on the agency. During this time a good trainer will try to expose the "new guy" to as many different types of calls as possible to help him gain confidence. Eventually, the new guy has to make decisions on his own of a practical, tactical, and legal nature in a wide variety of circumstances.

It is also during this time that new officers usually undergo another adjustment in the way they see the world. Speaking for myself, I entered this line of work with what I believed to be a fairly accurate understanding of human nature. I had worked with people in the past and knew something of what made them tick. I knew that the world was full of evil. I knew that people were selfish, manipulative, mean, and greedy. I knew that people protected themselves at all costs and lied to get out of trouble. I knew people drank and used drugs and then got out of control. I knew that many people held a distaste for rules and for those who enforced them. I had seen all these things before.

Yet, as well prepared as I was to face more evil, I was astonished. It is one thing to know that people are violent toward their family but it is a different thing to see it happen and put faces to it. I did not grow up with violence in my home and there certainly is none in my own family now. So it became real to me when I walked into a house where a young woman, about twenty years old, had stabbed her boyfriend. These were real people and now I was meeting them. I was hearing them yell in pain, asking, "Why did you do this to me?" I was seeing their anger and fear. I was smelling their blood.

I walked into homes where no one ever cleaned anything. Not the floor, not the counter, not the dishes, not the toilet. Nothing. Ever. You do not know that smell until you have been in a house like that.

I met women who made every possible excuse for the abuse that their boyfriends dealt them. They all told me that he was a really good dad and a really nice guy when he was sober. Love is a strange thing.

I met people who had served time in prison for sexually abusing children and now they were breaching the terms of their release. Why did we let this guy out of prison in the first place?

I walked into homes bursting with despair, where teen-agers or fathers of young children had taken their own lives. I walked into homes where husbands had lost wives, children had lost parents, or parents had lost children.

Perhaps you already see the point. If any of us were hired with even a small part of our innocence intact, it was demolished after a few months on the streets. For hours on end each day, I found myself wading through the evidence and remains of someone else's bad decisions and gut-wrenching pain.

It did not take long to notice something else. I began hearing the same names over and over again. I began meeting people for a second time, then a third time. It quickly became clear that police were spending the vast majority of their time dealing repeatedly with a tiny fraction of the population.

Perhaps you are one of those who have never really interacted with police aside from occasionally being pulled over in your car. Do not be fooled into thinking that the police are not busy. There are others in your city who do more than make up for your good behaviour.

As I got to know those with whom we interacted most frequently, I saw why police officers can get so jaded. Not only was I walking through the ruins of human lives, I would see those humans making the same mistakes over and over. I got to know their family situations and saw the hopelessness that surrounded them.

I learned about chronic domestic issues because we would respond at least once every month to the same residence. I met people with mental health and addiction issues, things that seemed impossible to overcome.

I saw people treat other people in ways I would not even treat a rodent (and I am no fan of rodents).

The Alternate Dimension

Over time I saw that there was a certain segment of the population who simply did not fit into society in the usual way. What I mean is that for some, the rules of society—written and unwritten—were either unknown or ignored. They came from various backgrounds, races, and cultures but what they had in common was that they were lost. They were adrift in life without a moral compass, with little or no stability in their family lives, and no religious beliefs or social bonds to anchor them. Their lives were lived by a different code, an alternative way of interacting with the world around them. Every day that I went to work I found I was in a different world, an alternate dimension to the one in which I lived.

Somewhere near you are the people who live in that alternate dimension. You see them when you watch a man pushing a shopping cart full of garbage bags along the sidewalk. You see them when you watch someone stumbling down the street intoxicated on a Tuesday morning. These are the people who live by another code.[2]

Several problems seem to be common among those who follow this code. For one thing, many have life skills and problem-solving abilities that are surpassed by most ten-year-old children. There are people who phone the

---

2 For a much more academic treatment of this topic I would suggest reading from the collection of essays by Theodore Dalrymple, *Life at the Bottom: The Worldview That Makes the Underclass* (Chicago: Ivan R. Dee, 2001).

police because their wife did not make them dinner, their cousin is glaring at them from across the room, or their brother drank the last beer in the fridge. They have not learned to deal with the small problems in life, let alone the large ones. I have seen an adult smash a giant bottle full of hard liquor on the ground in anger because the alternative was to share it with someone else—and he would rather have it all.

Just as common is the fact that the people of the alternate dimension are poor, uneducated, and most do not work consistently or at all. But it's not as simple as saying they should be given more money, better education, and full-time jobs. When I meet them and hear their stories it seems that by trying to push such solutions people are mistaking the effect for the cause.

From the start, I found that I was not meeting the first generation to fall into this alternate dimension. I saw strong evidence that this was generational. Somewhere in the past, the rest of society left some people behind. But why was that? Eventually I came to believe that I could narrow it down to two significant things that the people had in common, things that might be closer to the root cause: addiction and broken familial relationships. Nearly every person I have met who's lived in that alternate dimension has suffered from at least one, but usually both, of these problems.

Witnessing these lives up close, it's easy to see how the cycle is perpetuated. Put simply, addiction destroys families. Addiction diminishes problem-solving skills and intellectual function. The children raised in these broken homes riddled with addiction are often ill-prepared for the world with its social and intellectual requirements. Very often, people raised without stable, caring familial authority figures fall into addiction (as demonstrated by their only role models, their family members with addictions) and they search for basic social fulfillment in bad company. This terrible cycle carries on until—rarely and through some miracle—it is broken by an exceptional person here and there.

One of the things that is most bewildering about working in the alternate dimension is the fact that the people who call us most often are the very same people who hate us the most. They phone the police in a panic because someone has bothered them, and when we arrive they despise our presence, lock us out of their homes, swear at us, and give us the finger. I do not know how many times I have thought to myself, or said aloud, "But, YOU called US!"

Soon enough, some of the people I've dealt with at work are due for their day in court. This is where, early on, I learned even more about my new job and how it related to the justice system.

The Criminal Justice System
Have you ever played the arcade game known as Whac-A-Mole? A player stands in front of a table with several holes in the surface. A plastic mole will come up out of each hole. When you hit a mole with a mallet it retreats back into the hole. Every time you knock a mole back into its hole one or two more pop up out of other holes. So you continually whack the moles only to find that they return shortly.

I can think of no better way to describe how police feel about the justice system. We participate extensively in the justice system. We receive information from the public, we gather evidence, we identify, locate and arrest offenders, we attend court to testify, then we enforce the conditions placed on the offenders upon their release. And every time we take someone to jail he pops up again a little while later, with no improvement in his behaviour.

Before we move on, I believe it would help to provide a simple synopsis of how Canadian law is created and enforced.

How Laws are Made

The Canadian legal system is designed to have several entities playing various roles in the creation, interpretation, and enforcement of the laws. Initially, the laws are drafted and brought into existence by the politicians in parliament. After the laws pass through the senate and are made official by the governor general, they come into effect. It is then up to police to enforce the laws as they are written.

However, these laws are not static or rigid; they remain dynamic, changing over the course of time. The reason for this is that the court system plays a significant role in law making. In fact, I would argue that the court system plays an even greater role than parliament in shaping the way the laws of the Criminal Code of Canada are enforced. This is because after a law is created in Ottawa it is left to the courts to interpret that law. Sometimes, the courts will even strike down a new law at the first opportunity and declare that it was unconstitutional from the start.

For instance, in 2012, parliament passed the Safe Streets and Communities Act, creating mandatory minimum sentences for several kinds of criminal offences. These mandatory sentences did not survive their first challenge in the Supreme Court of Canada and, therefore, have never been enforced.[3]

As people accused of breaking laws appear before the courts, judges determine how they will interpret the laws. Every decision made in relation to the law becomes part of a growing body of literature known as case law. Case law refers to the precedents set by judges in past decisions and it is used as a reference point on how to deal with subsequent cases. Case law is considered authoritative as a general guide when it comes to interpreting the law, determining guilt or innocence, or setting a sentence.

Robbery With A Firearm

Take, for example, the charge of committing an armed robbery. Consider the following scenario.

A suspect walks into a convenience store with a sawed-off rifle, points it at the young clerk behind the counter and yells at her that he wants the cash and the lottery tickets. The clerk panics and backs away. The suspect walks behind the counter, pushes the clerk aside, and takes the lottery tickets. As the suspect leaves he yells, "Don't call the cops!"

---

3   Supreme Court of Canada, "R v. Lloyd," Supreme Court Judgements, April 15, 2016, scc-csc.lexum.com/scc-csc/scc-csc/en/item/15859/index.do

The Criminal Code of Canada states that a robbery has occurred if a person steals something and threatens or uses violence, or is armed with a weapon or imitation of one. The code also states that if a prohibited weapon is used in committing the offence the offender is to be imprisoned for a minimum of four years with a maximum of life. (A life sentence in Canada does not refer to the rest of the offender's life; it means up to twenty-five years.)

In this case, the offender stole the lottery tickets and presented a firearm to the clerk; this is considered a robbery. In addition to this, because the firearm has been sawed down and is shorter than the legal limit, the firearm is a prohibited weapon according to definitions found elsewhere in the Criminal Code.

Here is how case law will affect a sentence in this case. If this suspect is identified, located, charged, and subsequently convicted of robbery with the use of a prohibited firearm, the judge will consider the sentences that have been handed down in previous cases with similar details. Buried in the mountain of case law there are other scenarios. Some scenarios are similar except that the suspect actually fired the weapon into the ceiling to let the clerk know he meant business. In others, the suspect was wearing a mask to conceal his identity. The judge may find in the case law that in those instances the suspects receive sentences of only two years. The judge determines that the sentence in this case must be less than two years because the suspect did not cover his face or fire his weapon. Consequently, our suspect only receives a sentence of eighteen months. It does not matter that the Criminal Code of Canada states that the minimum sentence is four years. Somewhere along the way, judges considered this too harsh. They diverted from the sentence prescribed in the Criminal Code and have been doing so ever since. Case law, the previous decisions of judges in similar cases, indicates that eighteen months is sufficient.

The Legal System

Here is a good place to talk about other oddities of the Canadian legal system. For instance, prisoners serving sentences of more than two years are held in federal penitentiaries operated by Corrections Services Canada. The Corrections and Conditional Release Act of 1992 determines that prisoners are released after two-thirds of their sentence is served in order to complete the remainder of the sentence under supervision in the community.[4] This happens unless there are significant concerns for public safety or the prisoner has not already been granted parole earlier in his sentence.

Furthermore, case law has provided double credit for time served before a conviction. When a suspect has been charged with a violent enough offence he is held in custody until the court proceedings have run their course. The court system is backlogged and the prosecutors are overworked so it takes many months to get to trial. If an offender has been held in custody until his conviction or guilty plea he receives double credit for every day spent in custody up until the conviction. This means that if the

---

4   Government of Canada, "Corrections and Conditional Release Act," Justice Laws Website, November 1, 1992, https://laws-lois.justice. gc.ca/eng/acts/C-44.6/index.html

offender in our scenario waits nine months from the day he is arrested until he is convicted of his crime he is considered to have served eighteen months of his sentence. Therefore, when the judge sentences him to eighteen months in custody, he walks out the front door of the court room that very day. In fact, many offenders play a game of delay tactics in order to rack up as much double credit as possible before pleading guilty and going free.

In addition to this there is the plea bargain. It is common practice that an offender will be offered a plea bargain in all but the most extreme of circumstances. A plea bargain is a verbal agreement made between the prosecution lawyer and the defence lawyer in collaboration with the accused. The prosecution agrees to drop or reduce certain charges and in exchange the offender agrees to plead guilty to the remaining charges. As part of this deal, the prosecution and defence agree on a reduced sentence that they will in turn request of the judge. The motivation for the offender is that he knows the prosecution will ask for a much lengthier sentence if the case goes to trial and the offender is found guilty. The offender, knowing that he stands a very good chance of being found guilty, agrees to the arrangement because he will receive a reduced sentence.

In the example of the robbery, if the suspect pleads guilty to theft and possession of the prohibited firearm, the prosecutor may offer a reduced sentence that does not include any time in custody. If this is the case, and this deal is offered early, the offender may spend very little time in custody after giving a lifetime's worth of trauma to the poor girl behind the counter at the convenience store.

One way I have seen a plea bargain played out is in relation to a domestic assault. The accused assaulted his girlfriend while he was intoxicated. Police, including myself, attended and found that the girlfriend was injured and there was other evidence to suggest that the assault had taken place. The accused was also on court-imposed conditions that stated he was not allowed to consume alcohol. These conditions were put in place because the last time he committed a crime he was intoxicated. (Yes, there is usually a pattern.)

As a result, I arrested the boyfriend and laid two charges: one for the assault and one for the breach of the condition to abstain from the consumption of alcohol.

When the day came for the boyfriend to appear in court I was also there, prepared to testify if necessary. However, my testimony was not required. Just before court began, the lawyers and the boyfriend agreed on a plea bargain. The boyfriend pled guilty to breaching his condition not to consume alcohol, but the charge of assaulting his girl-friend was dropped. And would you like to know what kind of sentence was imposed? The boyfriend was released on the condition that he abstain from the consumption of alcohol. This same condition, you may recall, was already in place the night he got drunk and slugged his girlfriend. This condition meant nothing to him then and it will not dictate his behaviour in the future.

In fact, many of the people who are in court on a regular basis are addicted to alcohol or other drugs, so telling them not to drink is pointless. However, that is exactly what the courts do, releasing people back into the community on a promise to stop doing something that they will likely never stop doing.

Lastly, a word must be said about those people who reject the plea bargain and go to trial. It is rare for someone to argue at trial that they did not commit the deed for which they were charged. Several elements of Canadian law, the Charter of Rights and Freedoms, and case law have provided people with many possible defences to present to the courts. For example, consider the ways people have argued their impaired-driving charges. Defence lawyers have attacked the integrity of the machines used to measure blood-alcohol content, the frequency with which the machines are maintained, the time it takes to administer the breath tests, the urgency with which police officers transport the drivers to where the breath machines are, and the order in which the drivers are read their legal rights and the demand to provide a breath sample. It is very common for the accused to argue that some event in the process happened out of order, or some uncontrollable circumstance kept them from exercising their rights, demonstrating the entire investigation to be a sham and releasing them of any responsibility for their actions.

The courts have allowed many forms of defence to be argued successfully because they consider it much worse to put an innocent person in jail than to let a guilty person go free. Of course, in principle, I would agree. The stories of those who are wrongfully convicted are heartbreaking. Where I believe the courts have erred (if I may be so bold) is when they have abandoned the pursuit of justice—the search for truth—in favour of an academic exercise wherein people argue over the rights of the accused and whether or not some breach of those rights should release him from being held responsible for a crime. Something tells me that if the judiciary was half as concerned for truth and public safety as they were for the rights of the accused they would keep more people in custody.

For this reason, the police continue playing the real-life game of Whac-A-Mole as people addicted to substances, people addicted to child pornography, people prone to violence, and people who show no regard for another person's well-being or possessions are released back into our communities. This elevates the level of danger, not only to the police officers who must track down armed career criminals, but to regular citizens who unknowingly drive the same streets, walk the same shopping malls, and eat in the same restaurants with those criminals.

Whac-A-Mole Continued

Let's now take a look at the role of the police in the story of the convenience store robbery. The police were the ones who received the frantic call on the phone stating that the robbery had taken place. The police responded and took statements from the clerk and from other witnesses. They examined the scene and searched the area for evidence. They found some of the stolen lottery tickets on the ground. They processed the lottery tickets for fingerprints and identified a suspect. They collected a copy of the video camera footage. They studied the footage and saw that the suspect appeared to be the same person whose fingerprint was found on the lottery ticket. They searched for the suspect and located him. They arrested the suspect, housed him overnight, fed him, and transported him to court. They wrote notes and reports to document their work.

By this time the police have collectively spent between fifteen and twenty working hours on this case over the course of at least one week. And this is likely the best case. It is rare for a suspect to be held in custody until trial. Most are released under some type of conditions. In my experience these documents mean absolutely nothing to most offenders and little more to the courts. They are merely something that the courts can point to and say that they did what they could to avoid further catastrophe.

As a result, if the offender in our scenario is released the police may find themselves arresting him for another offence, sometimes another violent offence, before they have even finished their work on the first robbery.

This reality is played out daily in many different ways. I will share another true story from my own experience. Early in my career several officers spent a large portion of a night shift in an effort to arrest a dangerous person. We knew the person was inside a residence and he had warrants for several charges. In fact, he had warrants for more than a dozen charges. This was not a chocolate bar thief. This guy was a significant member of a street gang and he had a history of violent offences.

After hours of work, and nearing the end of our night shift, we had him in custody. He was to appear before a judge in court later that morning. Feeling I had contributed to keeping the good people of my city safe, I went home to sleep.

Less than fifteen hours after the arrest, I saw this person again. I did not see him in court or in jail; I saw him in a restaurant. He had been released by the judge while I was sleeping that morning and he was now dining with his friends and enjoying himself. This was a moment that stuck out in my mind, the moment I learned how the system worked. It also informed my understanding of what my hard work was worth to the court system. And it made me wonder if the average citizens knew how many dangerous people were moving freely in their cities.

The fact is that most people who are arrested for a crime are released back into the community within a few hours, if not immediately. The chart on the following page is an illustration of the various ways a person can enter police custody and subsequently be released.

METHODS OF RELEASE FROM POLICE CUSTODY

Type of Custody	Release	Timeframe	Explanation
Investigative Detention	Verbal	Immediate	Detention is a temporary situation in which a police officer keeps a person from leaving until a very specific investigation is finished. This last minutes.
Arrest (no charges)	Verbal	Minutes or hours	Often police have a good reason to arrest someone but soon find that there is not enough evidence to lay a charge. The person is released immediately.
Arrest (minor offences)	Appearance Notice or Recognizance	Minutes or hours	A person is charged with an offence such as theft and no conditions of release are imposed on him. He simply receives paperwork and promises to attend court.
Arrest (violent offences)	Officer's Undertaking	Hours or overnight	A person is charged with an offence such as domestic assault. He is released almost immediately, or once he is sober. He receives paperwork with conditions (such as having no contact with his victim) and promises to attend court at a later date.

Type of Custody	Release	Timeframe	Explanation
Arrest (more violent offences)	Justice of the Peace	Hours or overnight	A person is charged with an offence such as a robbery. He is held until the next opportunity to appear before the Justice of the Peace (typically available at least once every day). He is released after a bail hearing in the police station, with conditions imposed by the justice, and promises to attend court at a later date.
Arrest (even more violent offences)	Court	Hours or until the next business day	A person is charged with a violent offence such as a home invasion and has a history of violent offences. He is held until the next opportunity to appear before a judge in court, which at the longest would be over the weekend. He is released by the judge and promises to attend court at a later date.
Arrest (yet more violent offences)	Not released	Weeks or months	A person is charged with an extremely violent offence such as attempted murder. He appears before the judge in court and the prosecution opposes his release. The judge remands the person until a later bail hearing or, in some cases, until the person is either convicted or acquitted.

Manipulation of the System

I remember times early in my career when I would walk into houses in the middle of the night to find children wide awake and watching horror movies. Initially I was surprised that they were awake at two o'clock in the morning but I soon learned not to be so surprised. I also got over the fact that they were completely unfazed by movies that would scare many adults. What I realized next was the fact that the kids did not notice me walk into the room. It was commonplace for them that police would be in their home. What a life!

The people who regularly interact with police often learn a lot about policing. They learn how we do our investigations because they have been named in many of them. They learn what makes us move fast and what does not. They learn which words they need to say to accomplish the desired outcome. Long story short, they learn to manipulate us.

For instance, many people have learned that if they say they want their intoxicated friend kicked out of their house the police will come on their own time because they are busy taking care of more pressing matters. However, they also know that if they say their intoxicated friend has a knife and he is threatening people with it, the police will come immediately. I cannot recall how many times this trick has been pulled. Sometimes we're certain of this is before we even get to the house, but we hurry anyway because we cannot be sure until we arrive. Not only does this divert resources from more pressing matters, it also adds an element of danger because we break traffic laws to quickly respond to someone who does not really need help.

People also learn to use police as a weapon against one another. One of the common ways this happens is in a domestic setting. There are many factors at play in homes where domestic abuse occurs. It can seem simple from the outside but the reality is that it is difficult for people to escape a bad situation. The following is merely a scenario that has its roots in a thousand real-life circumstances.

A boyfriend and girlfriend are living together and have a child. One evening the boyfriend has too much to drink, like he has every other day that week, and the girlfriend confronts him about it. They argue and he hits her once in the face. She phones the police and he is arrested for assault. The police take the boyfriend away but he is released the next morning on conditions not to contact his girlfriend or consume alcohol. He goes straight home, talks it out with his girlfriend, and they go on with life as they did before. About two weeks later there is another argument. She gets upset and wants him to leave. When he refuses to leave she phones the police, knowing he is not allowed to be in her presence. When the police arrive they find the boyfriend in the house with his girlfriend, which is a breach of his release conditions. The boyfriend is arrested again and removed from the house. However, by the time he is released from custody she regrets what she has done and has texted him, telling him to come home. By the time the initial assault charge is dealt with the girlfriend has no intention of participating in court. The charges are dropped because she refuses to testify to the assault.

This scenario plays out daily across our country and it is a predictable cycle in many households. One issue, of course, is that the girlfriend is not keeping her end of the bargain. Police officers are often frustrated by the fact that conditions put in place for her safety are ignored until it's convenient for her to ask that they be enforced. And while I myself have complained about this issue and tried to explain it to many a battered woman, I do recognize that it is not a simple decision for most of the women (and sometimes men) living in such a situation. Often there are financial and family considerations that are not obvious to the outside observer. Does she kick out her husband, the sole source of income for the household? Does she tell him that he cannot attend the birthday party of his four-year-old daughter? These are complicated issues but I raise them to demonstrate that the police officer's work-load is often increased by a person's selective cooperation with the law.

One more form of manipulation can be mentioned here. People often dial 911 only to lock their doors before police arrive in an attempt to keep them from entering the house. They call 911 in a panic over something such as a sudden outburst of violence from a friend or family member. Sometimes they call 911 simply because they know that person will want to run away from the police, which is exactly what he does. In fact, several other people in the house also run away because they worry that there are warrants out for their arrest. After the goal is accomplished, the person who called 911 no longer wants police in their house so they lock the doors and pretend they are not home. When police insist on speaking with them they claim they did not dial 911. After all, they also may have warrants for their arrest and they did not really want to interact with police either.

Workload

One surprise in my first months on the job was just how busy we were. Some people think we spend most of our time sitting around waiting to observe a traffic offence so we can write a questionable ticket. However, if you live in a city of any reasonable size, I can assure you that the police are kept busy enough and consider traffic enforcement to be a necessary evil rather than a boredom buster.

For instance, according to the annual report published on their website, The Fredericton Police Force had 109 sworn officers and answered 23,939 calls for service in 2021.[5] This amounts to an average of 219 calls per officer. In the same year, the Winnipeg Police Service had 1,355 sworn officers and answered 234,058 calls for service for an average of 172 calls per officer.[6] These numbers provide a guideline for some further thoughts. Here is the information that is not contained in the raw statistics.

Though the stated strength of the police service is a certain number, a considerably smaller number of those officers are actually uniformed members answering the calls made by citizens. I will use the approximate fractions

---

5   Fredericton Police Force, "2021 Annual Report," Fredericton Police Force, 2022, https://www.fredericton.ca/sites/default/files/fredericton-police/fredericton_police_2022_annual_report_english.pdf

6   Winnipeg Police Service, "2021 Statistical Report," Winnipeg Police Service, 2022, https://winnipeg.ca/police/AnnualReports/2021/AnnualReport.pdf

that I know to be true in my own city as an example. They will be similar for other Canadian cities.

In my city, approximately one-third of the officers are actually assigned to patrol duties. This means that if there are approximately two hundred calls per officer in the year, the number is actually six hundred calls per officer answering the calls.

Accounting for scheduled days off, vacation time, and perhaps a few sick days, the average police officer is likely to work approximately 1,930 hours in a calendar year. If, on average, she were to take the lead on six hundred calls in a year she would be averaging one call for every 3.2 hours.

However we need to take into account that the vast majority of calls are not answered by a single officer. A partnership of two people would have to average one call for every 1.6 hours. Now take into account the fact that many calls are answered by a much larger number of officers. If ten officers spend an hour at a call, they have still only answered one call, leaving the rest of the members on duty to pick up that slack. Keep in mind that these calls are not spaced apart evenly to allow for breathing time between each one.

On top of this, most officers working the streets are expected to do follow-up investigation on their own files and on other files generated by other areas in the police department. And do not forget that, whenever possible, the police should be enforcing the traffic laws, stopping cars, and writing tickets for traffic violations.

I have not yet mentioned that there are often days missed for additional training, long-term injuries, parental leaves, and other such absences. This raises the number well above six hundred calls per officer answering the calls.

What does this mean for the officer you see driving down the street in a police car? She is under pressure to do a lot of work in her ten- or twelve-hour shift. Meal breaks or coffee breaks are cut short or missed altogether. She is backed up on paperwork. She may go home late tonight.

All that being said, if you were to have a conversation with her she would likely tell you that she loves her job. Even though there are great challenges in her professional and personal life she cannot imagine doing anything else. Every day brings her new experiences and she enjoys the teamwork and camaraderie she shares with her cowork-ers. At least, these are the things I would say.

3. DRUGS AND MENTAL HEALTH

Walking out of the police station on a sunny July afternoon I find three of my coworkers having a conversation in the parking lot where the marked police cars are parked. As I walk over to join them I notice something. There is a young man, about twenty years old, running as fast as he can into the parking lot. In the short time it takes him to approach us I can see that his T-shirt is drenched and he is yelling for help. About fifteen feet away from us he slides to a stop on the loose gravel on the parking lot and screams, "Help me! They're coming for me!" His eyes are wild, pupils dilated, as they look in the general direction of the officers but do not focus on anything in particular.

I glance in the direction from which this young man arrived and see only light Sunday afternoon traffic.

"Who's coming for you?" my friend asks.

The response is a panicked scream. "I'm being chased by hundreds of people! Can't you see them!?"

Encounters like this have become all to commonplace for me. Methamphetamines have broken the minds of a lot of people in my city and it is my educated guess that this is what has happened to this young man. He is sweating, possibly because he ran farther than I realize but likely because he is overheating from hours or even days of non-stop drug use. He cannot focus his eyes on anything and he is seeing a crowd of hundreds of people that I cannot see. If I am right, his life is in danger and he needs immediate medical attention. I radio the dispatcher to request that an ambulance come to our parking lot.

As if reacting to what I said, the young man screams, "Noooooooooo!" and begins smashing the side mirror of the nearest police car.

My friends and I move toward him. He is skinny, just under six feet tall and little more than one hundred pounds, but it takes all four of us to tackle him and control his flailing limbs. It is all I can do to hold his left arm and keep my leg under his head so he does not smash it on the pavement as he writhes. By the time the ambulance arrives I am sweating too.

BECOMING A FIRST RESPONDER OPENS one's eyes to things that are out of sight for most people. One of the most staggering things to wrap my mind around is the efficiency with which drug addiction can bring a life to ruins. Some people struggle to fight their addiction, living in a cycle of being clean and then falling back into a habit.

Some never really get clean and they live in a spiral until their life comes to a premature end.

In keeping with the requirements of Canadian law, police take fingerprints and photographs, commonly called mug shots, each time a person is charged with a criminal offence. As a result, some people probably have more portraits in our computer system than they do in their own possession. Through these photos one can see the changes occurring to a person's physical appearance over time. Some people have twenty or more photos in the system. Not only can I scroll through the photos and watch them grow through their teen years and into adulthood, but I can also identify the time they began doing hard drugs. For some, I can tell which photos were taken while a person was clean and which were taken while they were using drugs.

Closely related to drug addiction is the issue of mental health. Conversations about drug addiction necessarily include conversations about mental health. There are few instances in which drug addiction exists apart from mental health issues. Addiction to hard drugs leads inevitably to mental illness, often permanently so. And many who suffer from significant mental illness eventually begin using drugs as a means of self-medicating. The two issues go hand in hand.

Occasionally it has been suggested that police are the wrong ones to deal with mental health-related calls. It would be fair to say that a sizeable percentage of those who are shot and killed by police are experiencing some sort of mental health issue. Each time this happens a lot of questions are asked and the blame is often placed at the feet of the police. The implication, if not the explicit conclusion, is that the situation could have been handled without any violence if police had not been there.

During the summer of 2020 there was an explosion of anti-police demonstrations in the United States, many of which lead to deadly riots lasting for weeks. This brought to the forefront a theme never before widely supported: that police forces should be shrunk. People all over the United States repeated the slogan, "Defund the Police." I will address this issue in more depth later, but for now I want to focus on one train of thought surrounding mental illness that arose from this slogan.

As social order in the United States unravelled, many ideas were put out on social media—more out of emotion than actual fact. One suggestion was that there is no need for police to respond to calls regarding people addicted to drugs or experiencing a mental health crisis. Some said it was more appropriate to have addiction counsellors or psychologists go directly to the people needing their help. In fact, during that summer I noticed papers being written by university professors on this topic. They were not denouncing the idea, but rather they were trying to provide a framework for moving toward an actual shrinking of police forces in favour of other kinds of services.

I felt both surprise and fear when I realized this. I was surprised that someone as educated as a university professor would not be aware of the realities of crime, addiction, mental illness, and policing. I was alarmed that someone in such a position of influence as a university professor would be so quick to support an idea whose thinly veiled goal is the destabilization, not the betterment, of our social fabric.

During my time in policing I have heard a lot of naive comments and questions regarding the profession, but this one rates near the top. Please hear me out as I explain why.

Illicit Drugs in Canada

I need to pause for a moment to give a summary of the current situation as it relates to illicit drugs in Canada. There are many kinds of illicit drugs available for purchase on our streets. These drugs fall into several categories but in the real world they get mixed and sampled as cocktails of an ever more potent nature. Here is a brief description of some of the most common drugs that I have seen people using.

Stimulants: Drugs such as cocaine and methamphetamines fall into this category. Cocaine comes from a natural source. It must be grown and, typically, shipped a long distance before arriving in Canada. This makes cocaine more expensive than some drugs. The high that comes from cocaine lasts a short time, usually less than half an hour.

About the time I started policing, methamphetamines (usually referred to as meth) took over the scene. Police began seeing less cocaine and much more meth on the streets. There were several reasons for this. Meth is a synthetic product and it can be created using chemicals available at a reasonable price. This brings the cost of meth down and makes it more accessible. Anyone can learn how to cook it. Meth also gives users a much longer high. In fact, many people binge on meth, repeatedly using more before they ever come off the high. I have met people who have been using meth for days at a time. They do not sleep and they become increasingly paranoid over the course of the binge.

Meth has rocked the drug world in Canada. People who formerly used cocaine when they could afford it can now binge on meth for many hours for the same cost. One of the effects of using meth over time is the development of symptoms that strongly resemble schizophrenia. In the short-term this is often referred to as meth-induced psychosis. However, many who use meth will become permanently affected in this way. They believe they are being watched or followed. They see people, or ghosts of people, who are not real. They hear voices and sometimes receive sinister instructions from these voices. Even if they are still technically alive, meth has taken children, siblings, and parents away from their families by virtue of the fact that it has brought their thinking capacity to ruins.

Opioids: Drugs such as morphine, oxycodone, or fentanyl fall into this category. These drugs act as depressors on the nervous system. When used properly in a pharmaceutical context they are painkillers.

Fentanyl is a synthetic drug, created in laboratories to be used as a painkiller. However, the market for illicit fentanyl exploded worldwide a few years ago and Canada was no exception. This was in the news for a while before the media moved on to other things but the opioid crisis is ongoing. In fact, the year 2020 saw a record number of fentanyl overdoses in Canada. Ontario reported a twenty-five percent increase in opiod-related deaths between March and May 2020, compared with the same months in 2019.

Alberta reported that the number of opiod-related calls to emergency medical services (EMS) increased from 257 in March 2020 to 550 in May 2020.[7] Over the course of that year I personally attended the scenes of many such deaths. Usually those killed by fentanyl are in their twenties or thirties. It was hard for me to wrap my mind around it because these overdose deaths became so common that everyone who used fentanyl knew someone who had died. Yet the addiction continues to kill every day.

Mental Health-related Incidents

We must now return to the question of whether police are equipped to deal with addiction and mental health crises. When people say that the police should not be dealing with such issues, I agree in a way. Certainly there is other work that police need to do. Much of this work is not related to enforcing the law. But the idea that these situations can be resolved without police is unrealistic. It betrays a misunderstanding of what really happens. The reason that police need to respond is that it falls into their mandate of protecting life and property.

During their initial training and throughout their career police officers are provided with course material on how to deal respectfully and effectively with people in a mental health crisis. Of course, this material does not turn them into psychiatrists, but it does make them a little more aware than the average citizen of some of the issues

---

7   Vik Adhopia and Melanie Glanz, "Pandemic Worsens Canada's Deadly Opioid Overdose Epidemic," CBC News, June 10, 2020, www.cbc.ca/news/health/drug-overdoses-covid19-1.5605563

surrounding mental illness. The reality is that police cannot do more than try to safely de-escalate situations and then make sure that those who need professional help get that help.

The lie that is implied by those who would make addiction counsellors into first responders is that police are not suited to do even that much. The lie is that police are inherently dangerous to people who are in crisis and therefore someone else should deal with them. Some say that the instances in which people in crisis have died during an interaction with police are proof that police cannot deal with those situations successfully. However, the truth is that there is no one but a police officer who is capable of ensuring the safety of a person in a violent mental health crisis. The reason is that the police carry not only training and knowledge but also tools—the weapons on their belts—to save the lives of not only the person in crisis but also anyone else they may put in danger. There have been many times in my city when the police have used a taser to stop someone from hurting themselves or someone else. Yet those many successes seem to be overshadowed by the few times when a taser could not accomplish the job and a firearm had to be used instead.

When people started saying mental health professionals, not police, should respond to mental health-related calls the response around my workplace was complete incredulity. The fact that someone would suggest that mental health professionals become first responders to mental health calls betrays a profound ignorance of what it means when someone is in a mental health crisis.

I believe what people have in mind when they say such things is a calm situation. For instance, imagine that a wife and mother of two teenagers admits to her husband that her life has become too much to bear and she is contemplating suicide. This is the first time the wife has admitted her struggle to anyone. Having no connection to any mental health services, the husband does not know where to turn so he dials 911 and asks for help. In a case like this police will arrive to provide assistance. Of course, the police officers are not mental health professionals so they will refer the wife to someone who is a professional. They may even drive her directly to the professional at that time.

This is certainly one way that mental health calls can play out. However, this is not often the case. Experience has taught both the police and mental health professionals that a calm situation often becomes a dangerous one in an instant.

In many instances mental health and addiction crises are attended by violence or the threat of violence. Here are some examples of what a mental health crisis actually looks like:

- A twenty-five-year-old male is walking through the downtown streets carrying a long piece of metal that he took from a construction site. He is smashing the windshields of parked cars as he walks along the street. He is yelling incoherently, having a conversation with someone that only he can see or hear. If he encounters any real people he threatens them or chases them with the piece of metal.

- A mother of two elementary school children is running around her suburban neighbourhood streets screaming at the top of her lungs. She is completely naked. She is clearly angry at something but no one can tell why because the argument is between herself and the voices in her head. The front door of her house is open and her neighbours are concerned for the safety of her children.

- A young man barges into the home that his sister shares with a friend. The two young women who live in the house have several children each. The brother picks up a knife from the kitchen counter. He is convinced that someone is chasing him, though this is not true. The hallucination is a consequence of the drugs he has been taking for two days. When no one follows him in the back door he turns toward his sister, who is backed into the corner of her living room, sheltering four of the seven children who live in the house. Her brother yells at her that she has been following him too. She is one of *them*. She is certain he will attack her with the knife. Instead he puts the knife to his own wrist and slices through the skin, leaking blood on the floor. Then he runs out the back door again with the knife in hand.

- A husband and father of three has been taking cocaine for several days and he has become paranoid, convinced that the devil is chasing him. He has been hearing voices and the voices are telling him that his six-year-old son is the devil and he must kill him. He acts on the wishes of the voices in his head. In a frantic state, his wife dials 911, hoping someone can protect her son from her husband.

Any police officer working in a Canadian city could add many more stories to this list because these have become daily experiences. Here is the question that needs to be asked: Do you believe that a mental health professional or an addiction counsellor would be the most appropriate person to respond first to these incidents? I can tell you that the unanimous answer of mental health professionals and addiction counsellors will be a resounding, "No!"

Before you get the wrong impression, let me be clear. The people who are in a mental health crisis will indeed be brought to the attention of mental health professionals and addiction counsellors. But that absolutely cannot happen until the situation is made safe for those professionals to do their work. And no counselling can occur while a person is still high on drugs. A person cannot be counselled while she is still arguing with the voices in her head.

This is why the police respond first, in order to ensure the safety of any bystanders, as well as the person who is in midst of the mental health crisis. Only after the knives, guns, needles, and metal pipes have been taken away from the person can he be brought to the mental health professional.

Partnerships Between Police and Healthcare Providers

There is some good news here. Quite a few of the larger police agencies in the country have already developed working partnerships with their healthcare providers. In general terms, this allows for a mental health worker or addiction counsellor to be partnered with a police officer so they can provide coordinated service to those in crisis. These teams will often drive an unmarked vehicle that does not bring with it the stigma of a marked police car.

Of course, this does not mean this team is the first to enter into dangerous situations like the ones described above. That would merely serve to put the mental health worker in danger and it would not provide any extra assistance to the person in crisis. Rather, the team provides onsite service to some of the less violent people who come into contact with police, such as the woman who disclosed to her husband that she is contemplating suicide. When police are called to such a situation they will respond and find that everyone in the house is calm. The responding officers can contact the team comprised of the police officer and the mental health worker. This team can come to the house and take over the situation, freeing the responding officers to do other work. This allows for the mental health worker to come right to the person in need of help with the added protection of a police officer. The officer can keep watch for any safety concerns so that the mental health worker can concentrate on working through the steps the family will need to take in order to help their mother.

This partnership allows for a mental health client to receive referral to mental health services on the spot. The team can follow up with clients and work with them toward ongoing success. There is an understated value to this arrangement. Such a team is able to concentrate their efforts on people who repeatedly reach a place of crisis and end up dealing with police. This extra attention translates into fewer interactions with police because they do not reach that level of crisis as often. This means fewer situations that are dangerous to both the client and the police.

So you see, the police are already doing what has been suggested by some who call for defunding. Police have partnerships with professionals that allow for mental health services to be brought directly to a person in need. The caveat is that they do so only in the cases where it is safe for the mental health professional to work. And the police are best equipped to make certain a place is safe for them to work. The funny thing about this is that police actually need more money, not less, to provide services such as these. Any reduction in funding will see programs like these cut first.

What Happens When It Gets Violent?

Let's return to the question of why it is that some people have died while interacting with police during a mental health crisis. I would like to acknowledge that this is difficult territory for some people. This subject should never be treated lightly. Family members of people who have died at the hands of police struggle to understand why or how such a thing could happen. Many do not want to accept the explanation that comes out of the investigation. I understand that losing someone is very painful. Losing someone in such a way would add great confusion to that pain.

The other people greatly affected by these incidents are the police officers themselves. The people who go to work in my police station do so to protect people. We go to work each day willingly taking the risk that we might get hurt at work that day. We go to work knowing it is possible that we may have to hurt someone in order to protect another person. And while we recognize that these events happen in our world, believe me when I say that we hope these things will not happen. Not to us. Not today. Not ever.

But sometimes these things do happen. And when they do, each situation is different and the particular set of circumstances leading up to a person's death are unique. However, for the sake of simplicity I will divide these into three categories. In some cases police have to take action that ends the life of a person. In others the person dies while in police custody but as a result of something they have done, whether suicide, an overdose, or an accident. There is a hybrid situation in which people purposely do something to get police to kill them.

In the next chapter I will describe how police deal with violent situations generally. These principles apply to any situation in which police need to use force to control a person. Of course, an officer who is able to recognize that he is dealing with a person in a mental health crisis may be able to change his tactics if he finds that it will help calm a situation. However, there are some cases in which there is no possible way to secure a non-violent outcome.

More often than not, if the police take an action that ends someone's life it is through the use of a firearm. Officer-involved shootings are not commonplace in Canada, but they do happen. In many instances the person will go on to recover from the injury they receive. Occasionally they do not. Very often, perhaps in the great majority of cases, mental illness and/or drug use are major factors.

Let us return to the three reasons why a police officer may have to act and cause grave injury to a person. First, it is the general consensus among the police officers I have spoken with that a person who is sober and has good mental health will usually not do something so dangerous as attacking a police officer with a weapon. Even people who live their lives by a different set of rules know that this is foolhardy and is likely to result in their own injury or death. That being said, sometimes people do such things. They may aim a gun at a police officer, trying to avoid an arrest. They may even think that they have the upper hand and can shoot the police officer before the officer is able to defend herself. Whatever they are thinking, they make a very poor decision in that moment and the officer is compelled to do something she never wanted to do. When this happens, the police officer—in self defence or to protect someone else—acts to stop the person from carrying through with their apparent intentions.

The second category involves the death of a person who is in police custody that results from something they themselves did. There are times when police are called because a person's drug use has brought them to a place where they are out of control. One common form this takes is when a person enters a medical condition known as excited delirium. Excited delirium refers to a state in which a person's heart is racing extremely fast, their body temperature is rising, and they are often hallucinating. They lose touch with reality. This is the result of ingesting a large quantity of drugs such as meth, often over the course of days. Once a person has reached a state of excited delirium it is impossible to predict the outcome.

Some may survive the ordeal if they were given time to let the drugs run through their system. Others will not survive. However, because of the break with reality, they do something that draws attention to themselves. They may become violent and attack their own friends or family. They may go outside and yell at passing vehicles while walking down the middle of the street. Often they remove most or all of their clothing as their body temperature rises. Some are on a collision course with death and the only thing that will save their lives is medication that counteracts the effect of the drugs. This medication has to be delivered through an injection.

I have been involved in several incidents of this sort. Once a person is in a state of excited delirium it usually takes five or six strong people to gain control of the individual. The strength of an excited delirium patient is off the charts. Because of the break with reality they cannot even hear what they are being told, let alone comply with any instructions. So they need to be wrestled into a position in which a medical professional, typically an emergency medical technician (EMT), can safely inject them with the medication to slow their heart rate.

People in this state are usually not beyond help and I have seen this medication work numerous times. However, on some occasions, people have simply ingested too many drugs and their hearts quit. Once a person has reached this place, there is little that can be done for them. An EMT cannot be expected to inject medication before a person is under control. They will only get themselves hurt. And a person who is in a state of excited delirium cannot be controlled without some degree of force.

The results of a study on excited delirium, undertaken by a group of medical experts, is worth quoting at length:

> Given the irrational and potentially violent, dangerous, and lethal behavior [sic] of an ExDS [Excited Delirium Syndrome] subject, any [law enforcement officer] interaction with a person in this situation risks significant injury or death to either the [law enforcement officer] or the ExDS subject who has a potentially lethal medical syndrome. This already challenging situation has the potential for intense public scrutiny coupled with the expectation of a perfect outcome. Anything less creates a situation of potential public outrage. Unfortunately, this dangerous medical situation makes perfect outcomes difficult in many circumstances.[8]

The third category of people who die at the hands of police involves people purposely manipulating the police in order to cause their own death. If a person has decided on this manner of death it will be very difficult for police or anyone else to talk him out of that decision. This may happen quickly, as someone approaches a police

---

8 American College of Emergency Physicians Excited Delirium Task Force, "White Paper Report on Excited Delirium Syndrome," Academia, September 10, 2009, https://www.academia.edu/1131068/ ACEP_Excited_Delirium_White_Paper_Contribution_via_CA_Hall_ MD_FRCPC.

officer with a weapon in order to provoke a response. Or perhaps the person will take a hostage and threaten that person's safety in order to force police to act to protect the hostage. There are officers who take training specifically for the purpose of negotiating through situations like this. In these circumstances they will do everything in their power to resolve the situation peacefully. But it may be impossible. Police cannot make decisions for the person with whom they are interacting. Police can only respond to what the person is doing. Unfortunately, if that person is harming or threatening to harm another person then the officer will reach a point where he believes he must act. It is the responsibility of the police officer to protect the hostage who is in imminent danger.

This puts the police officers in a very difficult position. Presumably, the outcry would be louder if we failed to act and allowed the hostage to die. If someone tries to hurt or kill another person we are expected to act in order to stop this behaviour, even if our action ends the life of the person who put us in that position.

I have been in a situation that nearly ended this way. A person whose drug addiction had eroded his mind got into a huge fight with his family. When the police were called, he announced his intention to get the police to shoot him. He came outside to meet us on the lawn, bringing with him a weapon and a defenceless member of his own family. I am thankful that he backed down after a short but very tense interaction. I knew that if he made a move to hurt his own family member I would have ended one life in order to save another.

Stop Asking Whose Fault It Is

Sometimes bad stuff happens. If I had killed the person who threatened to hurt his own family member on that day, I am sure people would have wanted someone to blame. Some would have blamed me. I would have blamed him. Others would have blamed his psychiatrist. But none of the blaming would have changed what happened. The real question is how did we get here and what, if anything, might be changed to make this less likely to happen again?

Years ago those considered mentally ill were simply housed together in asylums. Of course, this did a great disservice to many people and I would not suggest we return to that system as it existed. However, what has happened in the wake of closing down dedicated mental health facilities is that many people are living in the community with severe mental illnesses. I am not referring to people who live well with managed forms of depression or compulsive disorders. I am referring to people who have lost connection with reality. Some people are okay while they are sober but are in a state of psychosis when they are using drugs. Others live full-time in their own reality that is not well connected to ours. But the healthcare system is unable to find full-time or long-term help for them. No one is forced to stop doing drugs and very few people are forced to take their medication. Those few who are forced to take their medication are often given strict instructions to see the doctor at certain intervals to receive an injection. When they do not go to the doctor voluntarily it is the police who are called upon to locate that individual and bring him to the doctor. The delay involved in this process sometimes means the person has already reached the point of break down before the police find him and he fights with police.

Until we find a way to keep people from walking the streets under a drug-induced psychosis, the police will be called because people in this state very often become a danger to the public. Until we come up with workable solutions to violent mental health issues the police will continue to be the ones who respond to calls about people in mental health crises, simply because there is an element of danger to these calls.

As a society we value personal privacy, freedom, and liberty, and this is reflected in the laws of our country. What this means in practical terms is that people have the right to stay home and not take their anti-psychotic medication, or to mix that medication with alcohol and other drugs. We do not have much recourse to force an individual into long-term solutions. Eventually, some people who suffer from mental illness will find a lethal combination of illness, drugs, alcohol, and/or weapons, and they will perform unspeakable acts. Some may die during the ensuing interaction with police. It needs to be understood that a lot of things occur to lead that person to the state they are when police arrive. There is a long road, perhaps over the course of years, that brings that person to the point of no return. Since lethal force is always a last resort for a police officer, the questions that need to be asked when these things happen are not about what the police could do differently. The questions that need to be asked are about what preceded the police involvement. It is often too late long before the police arrive.

Police officers would rather not be addiction counsellors or social workers. We would agree wholeheartedly that there are better uses for our time. But the ills of society and the lack of funding and treatment options for mental illness force us into these roles. As long as there is violence in the home, as long as people choose anger and hate over communication and civility, as long as families are broken up leaving kids without an anchor, as long as there are drugs such as meth, cocaine, fentanyl, and heroine sold in our streets and high schools, police will continue to play these roles. I see no other option.

4. USE OF FORCE

"Mommy, if a policeman shoots somebody does that person die?"

"No, my boy. They don't try to kill anyone. They just shoot the weapon out of their hand or shoot them in the foot so they can't run away."

"Oh. That's good. Then he never has to make anybody die."

WHEN I WAS YOUNG I had a conversation with my mom that went something like that. I have never asked her about it since. To this day I wonder whether my mom actually believed what she was telling me or whether she was trying to protect me from the truth. I suspect she believed it.

One of the most misunderstood aspects of policing is what happens around use-of-force encounters. "Use of force" is the phrase used to describe situations in which police have to take an action that may hurt someone. This covers a broad range of things and may or may not mean that violence was actually used to control a person or resolve a situation.

Any incident that is deemed to be a use-of-force encounter requires extra forms of documentation. This ensures that the events leading up to the incident and the incident itself are well documented, and the action taken is explained in detail. Many police departments will document somewhat innocuous events as use-of-force incidents simply to cover their bases in the event that someone complains of injury. For this reason, use-of-force documentation may be used when a suspect sustains a small bruise in the course of a foot chase. Sometimes police will use the same documentation even when a suspect complains that they were hurt by police but no actual injury can be detected. As the public grows more critical of the police they know they have to be more transparent, especially when it comes to these sorts of incidents. Of course, this means that any time a police officer uses a weapon of any sort, such as pepper spray or a taser, these must be documented as use-of-force incidents.

Police officers are conditioned to be vigilant in order to keep themselves safe. We know that people are unpredictable and if our training has not made us careful then our experience will. Things can turn violent very fast and without warning. This means that any call, any interaction with the public, any situation at all, has the potential to turn into a use-of-force encounter.

Police officers are often required to take physical control of other people for a variety of reasons. We remove people from parties after they have overstayed their welcome, we detain people in the vicinity of a street robbery, we place people under arrest, and occasionally we get into fights with people.

For these reasons we spend a lot of time familiarizing ourselves with two pieces of literature that provide a framework for what we do. First, there are sections in the Criminal Code of Canada that describe the legal justification for use of force. Second, there is a chart, known as the National Use of Force Model, that has been adopted in Canada to help explain the laws contained in the Criminal Code.

Criminal Code Sections

Sections 25–27 of the Criminal Code of Canada are the three sections that address use of force. The words in these sections are certainly applicable to policing, but the truth is they also apply to anyone who uses force to uphold the law, such as a security guard in a mall. In fact, section 25 specifically states that it applies to someone who comes to the aid of a police officer. We will go through these sections one at a time.

Section 25 lays out the groundwork for use of force in Canada. As a summary, the section states that anyone, including a peace officer, is justified in using as much force as is necessary to administer or enforce the law, as long as he acts on reasonable grounds. Furthermore, this section says that a person is justified in using force that is intended or likely to cause death or grievous bodily harm. However, that level of force is only justified if it is reasonable to believe that it is the only means of self-preservation or the preservation of anyone under that person's protection.

This section applies to a person who is doing something to enforce the law, is attempting to arrest someone who has broken the law, or is trying to prevent someone from breaking the law. Section 25 says we are justified in using as much force as is necessary to accomplish our goals when we are acting on reasonable grounds. The term "reasonable grounds" means that we must have a good purpose for acting, which we can explain to a reasonable person. Our explanation has to be based in fact, not merely in suspicion or dislike for a person. If there are good reasons to arrest someone, not merely a guess or a hunch, then we are justified in using force in order to effect that arrest.

Additionally, section 25 also addresses violent uses of force that can be expected to cause serious or fatal injury to another person. It states that the only reasons for using force of this sort are for self-preservation, or the preservation of someone else. Therefore, we are justified in using lethal force if we are concerned that what a person is doing will cause "grievous bodily harm" or death to ourselves or to someone else.

Section 26 states that anyone who is authorized by law to use force is criminally responsible for any excess of force used. This is simple to understand, but not as simple to apply because each scenario is unique. When this becomes a matter of dispute, the courts are supposed to take all the factors in the situation into account to determine whether too much force was used.

In cases where the court decides that there was an excess of force applied, the person who used that force is held accountable. This means that if I arrest someone and commit unnecessary violence, I can be charged criminally. This has happened to police officers. We find ourselves in situations daily in which we must strike a balance between keeping ourselves safe and not over-responding to the threat against our safety. At times it is a tough balance indeed. This is only made more difficult when we know that situations change or deteriorate into violence quickly.

Section 27 states that anyone is justified in using as much force as necessary to prevent a person from taking an action for which he believes the person could be arrested. This section clarifies that there is justification for using a reasonable amount of force for the prevention of criminal acts. In its most extreme application, it would justify a person using lethal force if it prevents the imminent murder of another person, perhaps a hostage. More commonly, it may justify someone in using force to stop one person who is planning to punch another person.

The Use of Force Model

The National Use of Force Model is used to explain the sections in the Criminal Code and how they should be applied to law enforcement. This model was developed by a group of use-of-force experts from around the country.[9] The model has been used in the court system and is a standardized way to understand and judge—as an academic exercise—the actions of police officers.

---

9   Canadian Association of Chiefs of Police, "National Use of Force Framework," CACP, November, 2000, https://www.cacp.ca/cacp-use-of-force-advisory-committee.html?asst_id=199.

Bear in mind that while this is an academic exercise, it speaks to real-life events. While the model has its place, it merely functions as a tool.

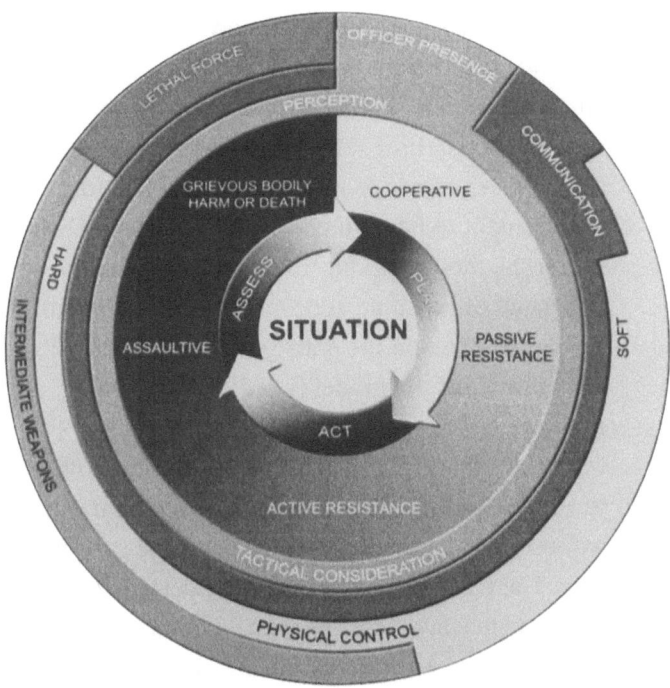

As you can see, the model is a circular shape, as opposed to a linear graph that implies a step-by-step progression. One reason for this is that physical conflicts are fluid. In an instant, a seemingly calm situation can skyrocket into a deadly encounter. On the other hand, a violent fight can end quickly if someone gives up and submits to handcuffing. There is rarely a clear progression or a predictable path around the circle.

Around the outer edge of the circle, in various shades, are the designations for police behaviour and response. As I explain the model, imagine us starting at the top and moving around clockwise. I will explain all of these below:

- Officer Presence: This designation is listed near the top and is consistent around the entire circumference of the circle. It goes without saying that police are present any time they are involved in a situation. Officer presence also refers to the fact that police ought to have an effect on a situation. Their uniforms, their weapons, their position of authority, will generally elicit an appropriate response from people. The reason the entire section in the top right corner of the model is dedicated to officer presence is that sometimes presence is enough to resolve a situation. I have arrived with other officers to a house party and watched the house clear out without having to tell a single person the party was over. The partygoers saw the police cars and knew it was time to leave. Most people, whether they like it or not, recognize that the police have been given a certain kind of authority and will respond appropriately to police presence. Before we move on, notice that the word "Perception" and the phrase "Tactical Consideration" are also included in the same circle. I will explain these later.

- Communication: Usually situations are not resolved simply by driving a police car into an area and watching people. Police have to communicate with people, listen to them, and help them resolve their issues. This forms the vast majority of police work and almost all situations are dealt with in this way. Police may arrive at a home where people have been arguing and a conversation is enough to calm the situation and find a solution to help everyone avoid further conflict for the evening. Notice that the communication circle also stretches around clockwise to the top of the model, indicating that as long as police are in a situation they should continue to communicate with people.

- Physical Control (Soft and Hard): Sometimes communication is not enough to resolve a situation. In these cases police may need to step in and take physical control of a person. The words "soft" and "hard" are at opposite ends of the next portion of the model. When police handcuff a cooperative subject they are already using soft control. No violence or injury has occurred, but the police have physically asserted their control over a person. This category also includes other actions that police may have to take, short of using a weapon, to take control of a person. Perhaps this means a short scuffle or a fist fight. I have had my share of wrestling matches with people who resist arrest. Such things would be considered hard physical control.

- Intermediate Weapons: This category refers to the various weapons police carry on their bodies, excluding firearms. Police carry things such as batons, pepper spray, or tasers to be used as tools when physical contact is insufficient to take control of a person safely. These tools are not used nearly as often as physical control. These weapons need to be used because the situation has escalated for one reason or another. Any use of these intermediate weapons will automatically designate the incident as a use-of-force encounter.

- Lethal Force: This category is the last stop in the list of options police have at their disposal. If a situation dictates it, police have the capability of injuring a person in such a way that they may not survive the injury. Typically, this is through the use of a firearm.

Place these thoughts to the side for a moment to take a look at the other parts of the model. The model needs to be seen as a whole.

Around the middle of the circle are various designations for the behaviour of the subject with whom police are interacting. The behaviour ranges from cooperative to grievous bodily harm or death. I will explain each of these terms below:

- Cooperative: This is self-explanatory. The subject may be a victim or someone the police are speaking with about an argument they had with another person. The person is fully cooperative. This may even be a suspect who is being arrested and hand-cuffed with no argument or attempts to resist. A cooperative person does not get into an argument or a fight with police.
- Passive Resistant: This refers to a subject who is not fighting with the police or running away from them. Rather, this person is simply not listening to the directions being given. Perhaps this is a guest at a party who is no longer welcome. When police tell

him it is time to go he simply sits in his chair and says he would rather stay.

- Active Resistant: This designation refers to a subject who is intentionally disobeying instructions. The guest who is no longer welcome at the party has walked further into the house or locked himself in the bathroom. This would also describe someone who is under arrest but is pulling her arms away when police attempt to handcuff her. She is taking specific actions to do something contrary to what police are instructing her to do.
- Assaultive: We all recognize a physical attack as an assault. If police tell a person he is under arrest and instead of complying he tries to punch the officer he is being assaultive. However, the term can also be used another way. Under Canadian law a person need not actually throw a punch to be considered assaultive. A person could be charged with assault without even having touched another person. And this holds true in the Use of Force Model as well. Consider a scenario in which a police officer has told a person he is under arrest and he should put his hands behind his back to be handcuffed. Instead, he turns and faces the officer then brings his hands up near his face and forms them into fists. As he gets into the fighting stance he has crossed the threshold into the category of assaultive. He has indicated his intention to fight.
- Grievous Bodily Harm or Death: This category can be misunderstood. However, it is a very important category to understand correctly. If a person's

actions can be reasonably expected to result in a "grievous" injury, then he has already moved into this category. A grievous injury may be something like a life-altering head injury or a life-threatening cut to the leg. Even if all police officers were also medical doctors, they could not know for certain the end result of any given attack. If I see a person hitting someone else in the head with a metal pipe there is no way to guarantee the outcome. It could be that the blows to the head will kill him, and every blow brings that possibility closer to a reality. Or perhaps his brain will be damaged and he will be permanently disabled. Perhaps he will only be concussed. Because I cannot know the end result, the last category refers to behaviour that is likely (but not necessarily guaranteed) to result in life-altering injury or death.

Lastly, there is a section near the centre of the Use of Force Model that refers to the situation as a whole. This is where the model ties together. You see the word "Situation" directly in the centre. Around that word are three others: "Assess," "Plan," and "Act." This relates to the words I pointed out earlier in the first circle: "Perception" and "Tactical Consideration." These words are important because they indicate that the situation is a fluid one.

Every time a police officer comes into a situation, she is assessing it as she perceives it; she is making a plan based on tactical considerations, then acting on that plan. This will be true if something occurs over a long period of time, perhaps while she is watching that house party empty into the street for twenty minutes. This will also be true if something happens in less time than it takes you to read this sentence. It may be conscious decisions made over the course of time and changing as the situation develops. It may be a rapid response based on a trained instinct.

Every police officer will have a unique perception of a given event. Speak with three witnesses to the same incident and they will describe it differently. This does not mean that two of them are wrong, but rather it means that they all perceived the situation differently. Perhaps they had different vantage points or different degrees of familiarity with the people involved. Whatever the case may be, the police officer has to assess her situation as she observes it.

As the police officer assesses her situation, she has to plan her response. She will do so based on her training, experience, and everything she knows about the circumstances. Her response is based on her skills and her abilities, how they compare to those of the other people involved, and the tools at her disposal. These are her tactical considerations.

Finally, the police officer will act. And even as she acts on a plan she may immediately find she needs to adjust that plan because her situation has changed in an instant.

The issue of perception can become pivotal in explaining her response to a situation. One may not understand why a certain degree of force was used until it is explained from the point of view of the person who used the force.

As part of this discussion, I want to reintroduce something I mentioned in an earlier chapter. As new police officers train for their career they are often introduced to numerous worst-case scenarios. Whether through videos or real-life scenario training, they develop an instinct that will pick up on danger cues. You can see what I mean if you go online and search for video footage of police officers being attacked or ambushed. For instance, once a police officer has told someone he is under arrest, the collective experience of the policing world dictates that it is wise to take control of that person as soon as possible. Many police officers have died because they failed to do so and the person who was supposed to be under arrest was allowed to return to his house or vehicle and retrieve a weapon.

Over time, a police officer's own experiences will be filed away in the back of her mind. Lessons learned the hard way are sometimes the most effective. These lessons form part of our perception, and make us wary of things that the average person does not think of as dangerous.

So what does it all mean?

When the Use of Force Model is looked at as a whole it provides a guideline for understanding when and why police officers do certain things. The model is shaped like a circle because real-life situations do not move up and down these categories in predictable ways. This is why an officer is constantly assessing her situation and acting on a plan to resolve it in the best possible way. The officer is also accountable for her decisions. However, she can only control her responses. The rest of the situation is outside of her control.

The behaviour of the other person is a significant part of what the officer has to assess. As a police officer deals with a person she is silently, perhaps unconsciously, analyzing his behaviour. Her responses to that behaviour are expected to be appropriate, based on how the sections of the circle line up with one another.

Stuart and Tim Take Charge

It may help to consider a specific scenario. Two burly police officers, Stuart and Tim, come to a house where Edward is no longer welcome. Edward is a fifty-two year old man who weighs a little more than one hundred pounds. Edward has had too much to drink. In fact, his friend Rita, who invited him over earlier in the morning, has come to realize she is out of alcohol and Edward is to blame. He has enjoyed more than his share and now Rita wants him to leave.

When Stuart and Tim arrive, they speak with Rita and confirm that she no longer wants Edward inside her house. Tim turns to Edward and tells him it is time to leave; he even offers Edward a ride home. Edward says he does not want to leave, he crosses his arms and slouches a little further into his chair. When Tim tells Edward a second time that it is time to leave, Edward says he would rather stay and have another drink. At this point, Stuart takes out his baton and cracks Edward once across the shoulder. Tim punches Edward twice in the face and yells, "I said it's time to go, Edward!" Then Edward is roughly hauled out of the house.

You would be right to think the officers' response was a little harsh and the Use of Force Model would agree. In this situation, Edward's behaviour was passive resistant, meaning he was simply not listening to the instructions the police were giving him. As the model would indicate, the police officers should have continued communicating with Edward or they could have taken control of him and escorted a drunken Edward to the door. There was no cause to strike Edward. And for the record, while this type of scenario is a daily occurrence, I have never seen a baton strike used to make a passively resistant person get out of a chair. I am merely making a point.

Let's revisit this story, but this time without the baton. The officers explain a third time to Edward that if he does not stand up and start moving towards the door they will be forced to carry him outside. Edward stands up, unsteady on his feet, says he would rather have another drink but if they put it that way … and then utters something incoherent (*mumble, mumble*). Wobbly on his feet, Edward makes his way over to the front door. However, as Edward reaches the door he starts to think he is entitled to another drink after all. Edward picks up his shoe and decides he will show the police what he thinks of being kicked out of the house. Edward throws the shoe at Stuart. He faces the officers and clenches his fists.

Here is where the model needs to be studied carefully. Look at where "assaultive" subject behaviour is on the model. Now look at the various responses that officers might be justified in making. The officers are present but Edward is not responding how he should to police presence. Nonetheless, how the officers carry themselves in that moment is part of the situation. And communication continues to be a part of this situation. The officers will respond, at least in part, by telling Edward that he must stop throwing things at them. And, of course, they will do something more about it. Two other responses are still available, physical control and intermediate weapons.

Remember that I described the officers as two "burly" guys. There are plenty of police officers out there, burly or otherwise, who do not need to resort to any kind of weapons in a situation like this. Edward, you may recall, is a slight man and he is beyond his best fighting years. He is acting out like a child throwing a temper tantrum. Edward is also quite intoxicated, so he is not a very skilled fighter in this moment. It is quite likely that Edward's arms will get twisted up behind his back, rendering his clenched fists useless, while he is handcuffed and carted off to the police car. Two strong and confident officers do not require violence or weapons to subdue drunk Edward. In fact, though it is entirely justified on the Use of Force Model, they may not need to use "hard" physical control because "soft" control will suffice.

Jenna's Unfortunate Morning

As I said, a police officer is constantly assessing the situation based upon her perception of it. In order to demonstrate the importance of this part of the Use of Force Model, I will tell this same story again. However, this time the characters will be described differently.

Picture the exact same scenario with two small officers arriving at the house. Jenna, a member for five years, is training Cory. Both are small people and Cory has only been working on the street for two weeks. Jenna, a perfectly confident and capable officer, knows her skill level and the limits of her physical strength. She knows she is not large or strong but she is confident of her ability to use communication in most situations or her weapons when necessary. In contrast, Jenna is not confident in Cory's ability. She has only worked with Cory for a few days and knows that Cory has not yet been involved in any kind of physical altercation while on the job.

In this version of the scenario we will also replace Edward with Evan. Evan is twenty-four years old, he is built roughly like an Abrams tank, and he likes to fight.

The situation has unfolded just like the previous example until Evan arrives at the door and reconsiders his situation. Jenna watches as Evan stops in front of the door and reaches for his shoes. All of a sudden Evan's shoe flies past her head. Evan turns towards Jenna and clenches his fists.

The presence that Jenna and Cory carry in that room does not equal the weight of that carried by Stuart and Tim. The difference in collective size and experience simply do not equal that of Stuart and Tim as they face off with Edward. Communication is still crucial in this situation and Jenna is about to tell Evan what she thinks about his decision.

However, Jenna is not likely to step toward Evan and effortlessly take control of his arms the same way Stuart and Tim could do to Edward. Evan has arms three times the size of Jenna's and he is six inches taller than her, outweighing her by fifty percent.

Here is where the totality of the situation must be considered. Jenna is not only perfectly justified in considering the use of a weapon but she likely needs it in order to gain control of Evan. In that moment, if Jenna, a smaller and weaker person, tries to step in and take control of Evan (not knowing how much help Cory will be), she is likely to get hurt. Evan has already demonstrated several things.

First, he is not going to be cooperative. Second, he is willing to assault a police officer (by definition he already has). Finally, Evan appears prepared to continue the fight and is capable of doing real damage to Jenna.

In this situation it is appropriate that Jenna gives Evan exactly one more opportunity to put his hands behind his back before her taser prongs fly toward him. And, for all the reasons listed in the previous paragraph, that opportunity will be very short-lived. There's no need for any negotiation and Jenna will not say please. This is a dangerous situation that needs to be controlled as soon as possible. Whatever Jenna does to Evan next is something that Evan brought on himself.

The reason I spend so much time on this story is that the Use of Force Model, like real life, does not offer an exact formula. Life is not that simple and, thankfully, the model reflects that. Every situation is different from the last. With tens of thousands of police officers in the country there is a very wide variety in terms of their size, strength, confidence, abilities, and experience.

In addition to what we have already discussed, there are many other things that need to be considered as part of the situation. In Canada, police officers work within a diverse set of conditions. Sometimes things like weather, topography, or the layout of a living room determine their response because they make up a significant part of the situation as a whole. It may not be possible to confront someone on an icy street in the same way as on dry pavement. It is not as safe to work beside a busy highway as it is in a field or a park. Perhaps there are kids in the room or a dog that may bite someone. Some officers are working in a large group and sheer numbers will be enough to control a subject, while others may be alone while the next available officer is an hour or more away. The totality of the situation must be taken into account if one is to understand why decisions are made and why they are subsequently found to be justified in court.

Decide, Quickly!

Police officers in dangerous situations have a lot of factors to consider. However, sometimes there is not a lot of time to consider the options. Incidents in the real world happen fast.

In the story of Jenna and Evan, Jenna has to decide quickly what she is going to do because Evan is ready to fight right now. Jenna already knows a lot about her situation. She knows she is in a small living room, cluttered with empty alcohol cans and furniture. She knows that she is with Cory, a brand-new police officer with little experience. She knows that another police car with two more officers is on the way, though she does not know how long it will take for them to arrive. She knows that Rita is now behind her, out of her sight. She knows that she is a fast draw on her firearm. She knows that her taser is a good weapon but it is not effective every time. She also knows that releasing pepper spray inside a house will hurt everyone and its effects only kick in after about ten seconds.

What Jenna does not know until this very moment is that Evan will turn and attack her. That is the new information she needs to process, and quickly. She also does not know what Evan will do next. Evan might turn around, open the front door, and run away. He might wait for her to make the next move, and he might charge at her and throw all his weight on her, tackling her to the ground and potentially knocking her unconscious as her head hits the floor. Perhaps Evan will attack Cory; people often recognize when a police officer is new at the job.

Jenna would be perfectly justified in pulling out her taser and instructing Evan to lay down on the ground or kneel for a more controlled handcuffing position. And the moment Evan fails to obey her instructions, Jenna would be perfectly justified in pulling the trigger and hoping that the taser makes good contact.

Taking all these things into account, do you believe is Jenna afraid? Does she believe that Evan could seriously injure her in a fight?

We need to remember one more factor in this situation. Evan is very drunk. We cannot know what kind of person Evan is when he is sober, but that does not matter now. Jenna is dealing with an intoxicated Evan and he is likely not the same kind of person that a sober Evan is. This means that there is even less reason for Jenna to hope that Evan will make a good decision in this moment.

Whatever action Jenna takes, she will be required to justify it later. She knows that, but she has to do something to protect herself, Cory, and Rita, who invited them to her house to remove Evan in the first place.

It is necessary to consider one more "what if" in this scenario. What if Jenna does not respond quickly enough or with enough force to stop Evan immediately? What if she fires her taser but misses or the taser is ineffective? Now Evan attacks. And not only that, Rita, also intoxicated, is upset that Jenna has attacked Evan (at least that is how she will later describe it in court). Rita jumps Cory, effectively settling the question of how much help Cory can be to Jenna. In an instant, Jenna finds herself knocked to the floor and knows Cory will not be any help. She gets up as quickly as she can but she is retreating into a short hallway at the end of which there is a bedroom. She can only retreat so far and Evan is approaching with closed fists, yelling at her, "You asked for this!" There is no room to maneuver. There is no escape. The taser is useless. Cory is no help. No one else has arrived to help her. What should Jenna do?

Here is where I want you to ask yourself a question. What goes through your mind when you read a news headline that states the police shot an unarmed man? The first thoughts that cross your mind likely betray your biases, whatever they might be, regarding law enforcement. Are you shocked that the police are so violent? Do you assume, like the news headline practically begs you to assume, that police are in the wrong? Do you assume that an unarmed man is never a dangerous man?

Jenna is now, without a doubt, afraid for her safety. She now knows that Evan intends to hurt her and he will certainly do so if he is not stopped immediately. She also knows that if she is overpowered, or worse, knocked unconscious, Evan has access to the weapons she is carrying, including her pistol and a lot of ammunition. Jenna is responsible not only for her own safety, but also for the safety of Cory, Rita, and the other officers who are on their way to the house. Jenna needs to deal with this now, before it is too late. None of this implies that Evan's life is not valuable. However, it may be that Evan is gravely injured in order to potentially save as many as five or more other lives. And it should be clearly stated that Evan is the one who put himself in this position. Evan is the one who has forced Jenna's hand.

The Movies

I love watching a good movie with an unstoppable hero. Jason Bourne can get into a fist fight with a calm, almost bored expression on his face. Jack Reacher can jump into a room and fire a pistol immediately, seemingly without aiming, past the hostage and into the forehead of the bad guy. Sometimes I wish I could fight like Jason Bourne or shoot like Jack Reacher.

However, I cannot fight like Jason Bourne, and neither can anyone else, not even Matt Damon. The fights in the movies are scripted. Further, when Tom Cruise plays Jack Reacher, he does not have to aim because he does not actually have to be certain he will miss the hostage. He knows that no bullet will exit the muzzle of his pistol. It is all pretend.

These are movies and, love them as we may, they are fictional. Movies give us an unrealistic portrayal of the justice-enforcing, bad-guy-fighting, murderer-shooting hero.

It may disappoint you to hear this but there are not many people who could make that shot past the hostage's head and into the face of the murderous villain while simultaneously jumping into an open doorway. And no one in policing would ever try because they know they are far more likely to kill the hostage than the bad guy.

In the real world, a fight looks a lot more like a fight you may have seen when you were in high school. It is just two or more people trying to hurt or gain control of each other and it happens fast with hands, boots, elbows, blood, and saliva flying in every direction.

In the real world, police officers know that they are held responsible for every single bullet that flies from the muzzle of their firearm. That is why they do their best never to shoot the hostage—whether on purpose (like Jack Tavern, played by Keanu Reeves in the 1994 film *Speed*) or otherwise.

In this section I will walk you through some of the education that police officers receive during their training. This is an important section and it contains material that police officers wish people understood about use-of-force encounters. I believe that if this material were made widely available it would help the average person understand why certain situations lead to tragic conclusions.

We are Regular People
Earlier I explained the process that one endures in order to be hired as a police officer. We also covered some details about the training that officers receive in order to prepare them for their first day on the job. Two things need to be said about that.

First of all, the training is invaluable education and mental reorientation so that the officer can take a safe approach to a dangerous job. Second, none of that education can change the fact that the officer is a human being.

Just like you, we have mortal bodies with brains and internal organs. We have adrenaline glands, bladders, and bowels. Just like you, our bodies react to extreme stress in significant ways. Most people in Canada have never had a gun aimed at them. Most have never had anyone try to stab them with a knife or a needle.

However, if you ever do find yourself with a gun aimed at you, your body will react in a predictable way. Your adrenaline glands will dump a ludicrous amount of chemical into your body in order to provide it with the energy you need to fight or flee. Your heart rate will instantly shoot higher than it does during even a strenuous workout.

The effects of these uncontrollable physiological reactions will vary from person to person. When police officers recount these incidents, they report a host of different effects, such as:

- Hearing nothing at all, even though there is lots of noise
- Hearing everything or hearing impossibly quiet sounds
- Visual tricks like feeling one could walk into the barrel of a gun because it appears so large
- Moments feeling like they happened extremely slowly or extremely quickly
- Tunnel vision, perhaps seeing only the knife and nothing else at all

For these reasons, police officers are never trained to shoot the knife out of a person's hand. It is not close to realistic.

When we bring this into the real world our training and our policies must be realistic. For instance, in the shooting range I can put a paper target about twenty feet away from me. The picture on the paper is that of a man with a mean look on his face holding a knife above his head as though he is about to bring it down and stab me. Perhaps if my mother was writing policy for my police department, I would have been trained to aim at the knife. In the shooting range it is certainly a possibility to hit the knife every time. Knowing that my foe is only made of paper, I can stand still and put bullets through the paper until there is only a hole where there used to be a picture of a knife. There is no harm done to the bad guy, other than perhaps a broken finger. But is this realistic?

It is not even close to realistic. The paper man is not moving any closer; in fact, he is not moving at all. He is holding perfectly still, allowing me to take careful aim and destroy his paper weapon. He is not drunk or high on meth. He is not yelling or making any attempt to hurt me. Also, I am tucked away in the shooting range where I feel about as safe as I can be. My heart rate is normal and there is no adrenaline running in my blood vessels. I have fired my gun thousands of times under such circumstances and there is nothing particularly stressful about it.

A Bad Day at Work

There are organizations that study the physiological reactions to use-of-force encounters. Experimental and real-life evidence show that a person standing well over twenty feet away from me is a very real threat if they have two things: a weapon and a plan.[10]

If that person suddenly starts running toward me and I realize that he is holding a knife, I am in real danger. The human brain needs time to recognize the danger, and once it does the physiological response begins immediately, pumping adrenaline into my system. My brain still needs more time to respond to the danger, deciding on the appropriate course of action. Once that decision is made, I initiate an action that I have performed thousands of times in the past, but never under the stress that I am experiencing right now. By the time I begin reaching for my firearm the person with the knife is only twenty feet away. My heart rate and adrenaline are already starting to do their work. If I so much as fumble once in drawing my firearm I stand a much higher chance of getting hurt badly. I grip my firearm and start to lift it out of the holster. I start to yell the words, "Drop the knife!!!" At the same time I start to move my feet, hoping to step away from the attack that is coming straight at me. As I am bringing the muzzle of my firearm upwards, the knife is ten feet away from me and closing. I can start firing while my gun is still on its way up to the position where I want it. I have slightly less control this way but I am out of time. If I act quickly enough, I have fired two shots before I can even finish yelling, "Drop the knife," and I have moved several inches to the side from where I was standing initially. By

---

10 J.D. Von Kliem, "The 21-Foot 'Rule' is Back in the News!" Force Science, September 12, 2019, https://www.forcescience.com/2019/09/the-21-foot-rule-is-back-in-the-news.

the time I have fired those two shots there is no distance separating me from my attacker.

And here is another damper on your movie night. People who are shot with a pistol do not get thrown backwards. They do that when they are hit by a car, not by a small-calibre bullet fired from a barrel about six inches long. So while I have done everything I can do by the time the danger has reached me, I have likely not stopped the danger. This fight will go on a little longer and I cannot predict what the assailant will do next. In fact, as I write this, I just watched a video online in which nearly this exact scenario took place. The officer, who already had his firearm aimed at the person with the knife, fired seven rounds at the suspect as the suspect charged toward him. I do not know how many of the rounds hit the attacker but he did fall down, for a moment. Then he got back up, jumped the officer, and took his gun away from him. It was terrifying to watch.

When this happens there is no shooting the knife out of a person's hand. Time will not allow for it. The human body will not allow for it. The real world is not like the exercise in the range, where I can shoot the paper knife from the paper hand of the paper person. The paper person will hold still so I can aim. My body will be relaxed. I will not have either of those luxuries if someone wants to attack me on the street or in a small living room tomorrow evening.

Here I arrive at another important question. If this scenario I just described were to actually happen to me, what do you suppose would be my goal in firing my weapon? Do you believe I am trying to kill my attacker? Do you believe I want to kill him? Do you assume that such a thought even crosses my mind before it is all over?

I have never fired my weapon at a person. For this I am thankful, because no one ever wants to do that. I cannot speak from experience regarding what happens to an officer who has been faced with a situation like this one. However, events very similar to the one I describe above can happen, and have happened to people I know—in less time than it takes you to read this sentence.

The goal of the officer in this scenario is not to make sure his attacker dies or lives; the goal is to make sure the officer, and the people he has been charged with protecting, survive. However, when the level of threat has been so elevated, the survival of the person who is threatening the life of another is a secondary concern to the necessity of ending that threat. This is why a police officer fires a weapon: to end a threat.

There is a saying you may find hanging on the wall in a police station near you. It also appears in various forms as the slogan for quite a few gun clubs. It reads as follows: "The only thing that justifies a peace officer to shoot at another human being is the overwhelming need to cause that person to immediately cease what he is doing. That need must be so great that it does not matter if the person dies as a result of being stopped."

Whatever the conflict, whatever the urgency, whatever the level of danger, the officer's goal is to put an end to that danger as soon as possible and in as controlled a manner as possible. Life—even the life of the attacker—is always important, but it cannot always be saved. There are times when a choice has to be made to prioritize either the life of a person who cannot be controlled or the life of someone else, whether that be a bystander, a coworker, or oneself. Police officers know that if they do not act decisively to end a bad situation it is possible that even more people will be hurt because of their lack of action. It is a last resort to shoot another person, but at times it is necessary. In those moments (usually in very fast-moving situations) it means choosing what appears to be the lesser of two evils.

Hear me loud and clear. Not one police officer I know has ever come to work and said, "I hope I get to hurt someone today." I find it hard to even imagine a police officer wanting to be involved in a shooting or a lethal encounter of any kind. And there are several reasons for this.

First, as police officers, we know that we will be judged by a high standard. We are familiar with the Use of Force Model and the legal issues surrounding use-of-force and lethal-force encounters. We know that if we are ever put in a situation in which we have to do something that may end a person's life, our actions will be analyzed in great detail to determine whether or not we were justified in taking the action we did. This is a great load to bear, and each one of us had to come to terms with this before we took this job.

Second, we are familiar with the experiences of other officers who have been involved in lethal encounters. They have to endure a long process of evaluation to determine whether or not they were justified in their actions. They fear they will lose their jobs and their reputations. They fear their families will look at them differently. They fear their own mental health will suffer as a result of the incident. They are usually ripped apart by the media, as well as irresponsible people on social media. Their families are subjected to unfair treatment. Their kids have been mocked or hurt by other kids at school.

In addition to all of this, the officer will live with the fact that he has killed someone. Regardless of his emotional strength, this is something that the officer will have to deal with in order to move on in life. And the memory will last.

No one ever wishes for this. To think otherwise is to forget that police officers are people too.

5. MEDIA

Because instant and credible information is required, it becomes necessary to resort to guesswork, rumours, and suppositions to fill in the voids, and none of them will ever be refuted; they settle into the readers' memory. How many hasty, immature, superficial, and misleading judgments are expressed everyday, confusing readers, and are then left hanging? The press can act the role of public opinion or miseducate it.[11]

— Aleksandr Solzhenitsyn, Commencement Address, Harvard University, 1978

IT IS MORE IMPORTANT THAN ever to address the issue of media fairness. I am only in a position to scratch the surface of this issue. My hope is that no one who reads

---

11 Aleksandr Solzhenitzyn, "A World Split Apart," The Aleksandr Solzhenitsyn Center, June 8, 1978, https://solzhenitsyncenter. org/a-world-split-apart.

this goes on to make the mistakes that many people make when it comes to media content, specifically as it relates to policing.

Historically, the media has played an important role in society. The media is expected to keep the public informed of the events and political decisions that shape our cities, provinces, country, and international community. We rely on reporters to do good and honest work to get to the truth and present it in an unbiased way. Once armed with the facts, people can make informed decisions when it comes time to vote in an election or address an issue of public concern. This is a way for people to monitor the actions of public servants and hold them accountable.

Does it seem to you like those ideas belong in the 1950s? It is clear to me that those days are behind us. By now we should recognize that our media, in all its various forms, has an agenda. If it was not obvious beforehand, some of the events of the past few years have driven the point home. Exposing all the reasons this is true would require a much more in-depth academic study than I can provide here. However, I do recognize that, just as there are pressures in my job that are unknown to people outside policing, I am willing to bet there are pressures on journalists that I cannot know unless I become a journalist. Certainly big media organizations, growing larger as they amalgamate, come with policies and board-room directives that limit the freedoms of the real-world reporter. I would welcome more information directly from those who have lived with those pressures, such as that provided by Tara Henley, a former employee of the Canadian Broadcasting Corporation.[12]

Social Media

I will try to be fair to social media, since I am asking you to be fair to police officers. The truth is that there are many fine uses for some of the social media platforms that are available. People use them to promote their small business or find high school friends. We can stay in contact with family even while living on different continents. Perhaps even more significant, social media has played a vital role in promoting awareness of issues like those raised by the #MeToo movement and fundraising campaigns for victims of war and natural disasters. The internet can be used for much good and for that I am thankful.

However, there is a dark side to social media. It can be used to feed overtly narcissistic personalities. People who seek attention in all the wrong ways and for all the wrong reasons find themselves quite at home in front of a computer screen. They love being linked to hundreds or thousands of virtual friends who will in one way or another tell them what they want to hear about themselves and about the world in which they live.

There is also a side to social media that is terrifying. Consider the pace at which information can be shared. This is both good and bad. Social media can alert people

---

12 Tara Henley, "Speaking Freely: Why I Resigned From the Canadian Broadcasting Corporation," Substack, January 3, 2022, https://tarahenley.substack.com/p/speaking-freely?utm_source=%2Fprofile%2F15756028-tara-henley&utm_medium=reader2&s=r.

to an imminent danger so they can take cover. However, the lightning-fast dissemination of information can also hurt people, especially when that information is mistaken or even twisted to serve a certain purpose. It would appear that even some of those who developed social media platforms have come to see the dangers inherent in their product. Several of them gave interviews for the Netflix documentary *The Social Dilemma*, which is worth viewing if you are interested in this issue.

Going one step further, social media provides a platform for every opinion. While I believe freedom of speech is a pillar of democratic society, I also believe that some opinions are more helpful than others. The online world allows people to surround themselves with voices that reinforce their worldview, no matter how out of touch it may be.

Perhaps you know someone who believes that the earth is flat. That person might believe there is someone who benefits from convincing nearly everyone that the earth is a sphere. Until recently, it was likely that this person was the only one around who believed these things and he may even have learned to keep such thoughts to himself.

However, thanks to the internet and to social media, many people who believe the earth is flat have found one another and the first Flat Earth International Conference was hosted in North Carolina in 2017. As a result of the worldwide dissemination of opinion-based "facts," there is actually an increasing number of people becoming convinced that the earth is flat.

For the most part, those who have fallen for this conspiracy theory have not been harmed by it. But it serves to make a point. Somehow we have created an environment in which the words of people who are not qualified to speak about a subject have been given more weight than the words of those who are qualified. If people believe that the earth is flat, they have to discount the stories of people who have circled the globe in space, flown to the moon, or launched satellites and space probes. They have to disbelieve the accounts of people who have dedicated their careers to space exploration or scientific research, people who are more than qualified to answer the question, "Is the earth flat?"

This phenomenon is an indicator of the power of disinformation. This is the conversation we absolutely must be having at this point in history as it relates to both traditional and social media.

Competition for Attention in Media

It appears to me that social media has been hijacked into an alternative form of news outlet. Ask around and you will be surprised at how many people get their news solely from their social media platforms. Good journalism is being replaced by baseless opinions and false narratives that are being shared at light speed online. This has also had an adverse effect on the traditional media. Some elements of the traditional media have played down to this level and chased the stories that are fed by misinformation and political motivation.

The news outlets are competing for business. They need readers or they will not sell advertising and be out of business. So when there is a story that can be used to initiate or prolong a media feeding frenzy they will be certain to use it to keep consumers interested. The result may be that attention is diverted from more legitimate stories. A lot of significant events happened in the world over the summer of 2020 but very little airtime was dedicated to them. Between the stories about COVID-19, hatred toward police, and the looming election in the United States, no time was left for the stories that affected millions in Hong Kong, Syria, and Africa.

What I am saying is that I can no longer read or watch the news and accept every story at face value. Moreover, I think that you should no longer do so either.

Now, I want to clarify that I am not a conspiracy theorist by any means. I do not think one needs to be a conspiracy theorist to see that the news is delivered with an agenda. This may be more obvious if you watch news out of the United States, but there is plenty of the same going on in Canada. News stories focus intently on issues that are deeply divisive. Perhaps members of the media would respond by saying that they are focusing on the issues that are important to Canadians. But if social media is your indicator, I would say that it can only indicate what is important to a few outspoken Canadians.

Reporters are Regular People Too

Years ago I had reason to question the accuracy of the media because I saw them get the facts wrong in straightforward stories related to my work.

The crime section of the news can be a fascinating read. People are drawn to these stories as they contain outlandish tales of infamous residents of their city. However, in my work as a police officer, I play a role in some of those stories. From time to time news articles have been written about incidents in which I was directly involved and that drove home some lessons about how I should read the news.

I noticed early in my career that the news releases provided by police departments—and the information available to the press—were limited in scope. This meant that when I read a short article about an incident in which I was directly involved, I found that there were many details missing from the story. The news would report that a person was charged with impaired driving and hit-and-run but didn't include how drunk that person was, what he hit with his car, and how he behaved afterward—facts I knew because I spent several hours with him. If the news reported that there was a significant assault and someone was hospitalized with life-threatening injuries, I knew what those injuries were and I knew the relationship between the victim and the assailant. I also knew that the whole thing was over an unpaid drug debt. None of these details were part of the news story. Of course, this is the nature of reporting on incidents when the police only provide a small amount of detail. However, it demonstrates that a limited amount of information is present in any news story.

Over time I began to notice that a news story would get some details wrong. Often these details would be inconsequential, especially when read by someone disconnected from the incident. For instance, the article might call someone a cousin when they were an aunt, or say Smith Street when the incident really happened on

Jones Street. No big deal; these are small errors. Reporters are people too.

But there were some stories where the reporting was completely unfair. This often happened when accusations were made against the police. There have been times when people made unfair or completely fallacious accusations against members of my police service. The stories in the news featured interviews and direct quotes from those who made the accusations but no one was interviewed who could offer another perspective on the story or point out that it was based entirely on falsehood or opinion. Part of this problem goes back to what I addressed in my introduction. Police departments are consistently scant on details. They wait for an investigation to be completed before making statements to the media. This is a good practice if one wants to avoid providing false information. However, it does nothing to deter others from providing false information to the media (with no fear of consequences, I might add).

These types of stories feed into the bias that the police are corrupt or that they pick on certain types of people. Suddenly there would be a protest in front of the police station, followed by more stories featuring more people telling more false stories (with no fear of consequences, I might add).

By comparison, when I read crime-related stories in the news I often find there are disclaimers attached at the end. I may read in the news that the police stopped a stolen vehicle after it tried to flee, and that during the arrest the driver assaulted two police officers and then the police found weapons and drugs in his possession. After all those details are provided, I also read that none of these claims have been proven in court or that all of these events are merely alleged to have happened. I suppose the disclaimer is true. After all, the driver of that stolen car will get his chance to convince a judge that there should be no consequences for his actions.

One might expect the same benefit of the doubt to be given to the police officers. However, in my city it is not. When the media provides a story based solely on complaints about the police, there is nary a disclaimer of any sort. The absence of clarifying information can lead the uncritical reader to believe there is truth to the outright lies represented in the story. I understand that the members of the media may feel they have an obligation to report on the things that citizens bring to them. However, they do a disservice to the reader when they let an opinion (or a lie) be expressed as a fact.

These kinds of stories have been published more than once during my time in this job. And when they were, I would often be familiar with the details of what actually occurred. Yet what was portrayed in the media was not even close to accurate. My friends and I were vilified for doing our jobs. Over time I learned to avoid the news for a few days when such things happened.

Smartphone Videos

One day my partner and I pulled a vehicle over in front of a restaurant. It was not a run-of-the-mill traffic stop. We had information that there was a firearm inside the vehicle and for that reason we approached this traffic stop differently.

Following all the policies and practices of our police department, we initiated a process designed for high-risk situations. We used a loud hailer to address the driver, a dog from the K9 section was barking, and our firearms were drawn and visible to the public. It will suffice to say we made our presence known to everyone in the restaurant. After the driver was safely detained in our police car I glanced up at the restaurant and saw about seven people with their smartphone cameras aimed in my direction.

"Great," I thought. "This will be on the internet before I get home tonight." Of course, it did not matter if the video ended up online. We did our jobs perfectly and everyone went on with their day safely.

Earlier I told you that if you searched online you would find many videos featuring police in dangerous situations. If you keep looking, you will also find videos featuring police fighting with people, tackling people, doing all kinds of things to people that may not seem right at first glance. What I want to explain in this section is the simple fact that video evidence usually only gives a small piece of the story and it will never provide the entire story.

The Incomplete Record

In any video featuring police interaction with the public there are obvious limitations. We can begin with the fact that the video does not provide the details of what preceded the recording. Before the video began there was a phone call to the police or some reason why police decided to interact with someone. Perhaps the police stopped a car for a traffic violation, or perhaps someone called police about a house party that spilled out into the street and became violent.

Whatever the reason police are there in the first place, that reason is not communicated in a smartphone video. But this information may very well be part of the reason why police respond in a certain way. The day we pulled the car over near the restaurant is a good example of this. The way we treated that driver might have seemed strange to people, but we knew something they did not know and their videos could not communicate that knowledge to their viewers. The video would only make it seem that we had it in for that driver.

Another limitation of the video is that it cannot record what it cannot see or hear. There may be things happening off camera or things said too quietly to be heard in the video. These unseen and unheard details may be important but they are not communicated to the viewer. In addition to this, the video may not be long enough or shot with enough clarity to show subtle details. Videos do not always show the level of sobriety or intoxication of the people involved, the bulges in clothing that resemble concealed weapons, or the subtle movements of a person that let the police officer know he is about to be attacked. It may appear that the police attacked someone for no particular reason, but if they were given a chance to tell you what they knew, what they saw, and what they heard, it may be more clear why they acted as they did.

We Know People

It bears repeating that as police officers we spend the majority of our time interacting with a small fraction of the people in our city. Often we already know the people we are dealing with because we have met them before. As a result, we come into a situation with firsthand knowledge. We remember the way the person treated us in our previous interactions. We remember the results of those previous interactions, and we remember all the research we did the last time we dealt with that person. We come not only with our own firsthand knowledge, but also with the cumulative knowledge of our police service.

For instance, consider a fictional scenario in which I am on my way to deal with a household that suffers from chronic domestic conflict. A couple and their two teenagers live in the house and the parents are going through a rough patch in their marriage. I was at this house last week and at that time the situation was resolved with no confrontation. However, when I wrote my report last week I noted that the police had been to the house five times previously this year. I also noted that on two of those occasions the husband was very confrontational with police and once spat at one of my coworkers. He was arrested and charged criminally at that time.

In this scenario, one of the teenaged sons knows the police are coming and knows that dad is in a very bad mood. The son starts recording a video the moment the police car pulls up in front of the house because he thinks his dad might put on a good show. Once again, the video falls short. Even though it may show the interaction between the police and the family from start to finish, it cannot tell you what I knew about the family before I walked into the house. It cannot tell you that I know the dad has spat at police before. It cannot tell you that my partner and I decided ahead of time we would not risk getting spit in our eye and at the first sign of confrontation we would take action to mitigate that risk.

For all of these reasons the police are often misrepresented in the videos circulating online or in the traditional media. This will be of particular significance when it comes to use-of-force situations. We bring to these situations our knowledge of the past and often that plays a role in determining the way we respond to an individual.

Seek Truth

There are many people who play fast and loose with the truth. They are quick to draw conclusions based on little information, and when available details do not confirm their biases they ignore them or convince themselves that those details are not true.

So consider that the content you receive from the media is not always accurate and never the entire story. Do not believe the bias. Do not forget that everyone is out to make a point. Learn to read objectively and learn to read between the lines. Become a careful and critical reader because if you don't, you may buy into a line of reasoning or a political movement based on fear and anger—not on facts.

6. THE IMPERFECT POLICE OFFICER

"This is ridiculous. How many more times will we come back here today?"

My sergeant and I are standing on the sidewalk in a light snow flurry. It is Christmas Day and we have just been called to Josie's house for the second time that afternoon. That makes four calls since yesterday morning.

Josie came into a little extra money this year and has been buying the alcohol for this year's Christmas gathering. Her family has been enjoying her generosity and her Christmas spirit but they still cannot help but argue from time to time. In fact, the more they drink the more reasons they find to fight. No one has been hurt and no one, myself included, is interested in having anyone removed from the party. It's Christmas after all.

But every time someone gets upset Josie dials 911. It is a habit of hers at any time of the year but four calls in two days might be a new record. My sergeant, a police officer since the early 1980s and a great storyteller, starts to reminisce.

"Back in the day we would have unplugged the phone and hidden it in her freezer so she couldn't call again." I laugh but he is serious. "Can't do that anymore," he says, as he turns to walk to his car.

EARLY IN MY CAREER I had the opportunity to work alongside some seasoned supervisors who had been policing since before I was born. Their combined experience was invaluable, their steady hand and calm demeanour were something to aspire to, and their stories of days gone by seemed to come out of another world.

There is no doubt that things have changed. Once upon a time police did many things that are no longer accepted by the public. For instance, a few decades ago a man who assaulted his wife may find himself getting "a taste of his own medicine" from the police. There is still a remnant of the public who remembers the old days and perhaps some who think the police still operate that way. But I can tell you that they most certainly do not.

Over the course of the past few decades certain legal documents and social forces have pressured police to become more transparent, more accountable, and more professional. Overall, these changes are for the better. The police need to keep up with the expectations of society while at the same time maintaining peace and working within the law.

The Charter of Rights and Freedoms

The Charter of Rights and Freedoms came into being in 1982 and it forms part of the constitution of Canada. As such, it is one of the more important documents, if not the most important document, in all of Canadian law. As part of the constitution, legal arguments often appeal to it in order to discard outdated or brand-new laws created in parliament on the basis that they do not comply with the standards that are considered the backbone of our freedom. The Charter guarantees certain freedoms to every person in Canada. It was written with the intent of limiting government intrusion into the private lives of individuals. These limits of intrusion are guaranteed to all Canadians and anyone living in or visiting our country.

Like any other law, the Charter is subject to interpretation by the courts. As I explained in Chapter 2, Canadian law is alive and it evolves over time. As the world changes the laws are reinterpreted. When cases arise involving subjects never before dealt with by Canadian courts they precipitate decisions that require interpretation of law. These decisions often refer to the Charter of Rights and Freedoms. A legal challenge to a court ruling that hinges on interpretation of the Charter will usually find its way to the Supreme Court of Canada for final say.

As an example, consider the fact that cell phones were not yet widely available to consumers when the Charter was penned. It took a long time before many people had a cell phone and more time before the advent of the smartphone. Once smartphones were commonplace, with high-quality cameras and lots of digital storage, they became a wealth of information about any person who owned one.

Police recognized this fact and began to look at the information on the phones of people they arrested. This was not true in every case, but it became a common practice to glance through the phone of people suspected of drug trafficking. Anyone actively selling drugs was usually using one or more cell phones and the evidence was easy to find in the call or text history. There was nothing illegal about this because the courts had not ruled on it.

Eventually, people who were charged with criminal offences began to base their defence on the fact that the police should not have been allowed to look at the information in their phones. They wanted the judge to dismiss the evidence found on the phones because the police should not have looked at the phones without permission. Over the course of time the Supreme Court weighed in on this issue and set out guidelines for the circumstances under which police were allowed to look at a suspect's phone.[13]

The Charter has changed policing to a greater degree than a person like myself can appreciate, as I have only been doing this job for the past ten or so years. But this example demonstrates the general trend. Many decisions out of the Supreme Court have placed limitations on police, especially in regard to the circumstances under which they may detain, arrest, or search a person. These decisions dictate things as specific as how long a suspected drunk driver can be kept waiting before his blood alcohol content is tested.

---

13 For one such decision see Supreme Court of Canada, "R v. Fearon," Supreme Court Judgements, December 11, 2014, scc-csc.lexum.com/scc-csc/scc-csc/en/item/ 14502/index.do.

In summary, there has been a huge shift in how policing is done in Canada over the last forty years. The Charter of Rights and Freedoms, along with its interpretation by the Supreme Court, have galvanized some of these changes into law.

Civilian Oversight

In Canada, policing is a matter of provincial jurisdiction. Each province has enacted laws to govern the way police conduct their business within that province. These laws establish a process for review of police conduct and, when appropriate, they establish guidelines for discipline. Canada also has a national police force in the Royal Canadian Mounted Police (RCMP). Each RCMP officer enforces the laws of the province in which she works and answers to the policies of the national organization.

Each province in Canada has also established an organization to provide civilian oversight for police. These organizations go by different names in each province. In Ontario it is known as the Office of the Independent Police Review Director. In Nova Scotia it is called the Office of the Police Complaints Commissioner. The federal government oversees the RCMP through the Civilian Review and Complaints Commission for the RCMP. These oversight bodies play similar roles in their respective jurisdictions. They receive complaints from the public, they oversee investigations into those complaints and, when necessary, they recommend or enforce discipline. However, not all investigations are initiated by the public. There are some incidents that are automatically investigated by this or some other body of oversight. Such an investigation will be initiated any time an officer discharges a firearm at a person.

These processes have been established to make certain that the police remain transparent. From my perspective this is a bittersweet thing. No one enjoys participating in an internal investigation. These investigations are universally disliked by officers who have experienced them. They are long and arduous processes. Everyone involved in an investigation, whether citizen or police officer, is interviewed and provides a statement. Depending on the situation, the officer who is the subject of the investigation may be concerned that some form of discipline will be placed on his record or, worse yet, that he may lose his job. An officer looks forward to an interview of this sort about as much as he looks forward to a root canal, even if he is only participating as a witness. On the other hand, as much as it pains the officers who participate in such a process, there are some significant benefits.

First of all, if a member of the public feels she has been treated unfairly there is a place she can go to be heard. Her concerns will be dealt with by someone outside the police department and she will receive a response to her concern. The old complaint that the police are investigating themselves does not hold water anymore. Investigations are overseen by people who are not police officers and provide the results of their investigations to the public. The benefit of this arrangement is that it gives more legitimacy to what could otherwise be perceived as a recipe for a cover up.

The existence of the oversight bodies keeps police officers on their toes. I work with some outstanding people.

Each day I go to work I witness the professionalism of my colleagues despite the constant scrutiny of the public and the harsh treatment from the not-so-fine citizens of our fine city. But we are human and sometimes the threat of a complaint is enough to keep us calm when we are tempted to lose our cool.

My conclusion is that, overall, the changes introduced to Canadian policing over the past forty years have been for the better. Police departments have written and rewritten policy to guide their members in how they conduct business in a legal and transparent manner. I can confidently say that professional and honest service is the norm in my workplace and I am proud to serve alongside my fellow officers.

Don't Take My Word For It

To demonstrate my point, I'll point out the statistics from two areas in the country and see how many complaints brought to the oversight bodies were found to be legitimate. In Saskatchewan, the civilian oversight body is known as the Public Complaints Commission. In the fiscal year starting April 1, 2019, and ending March 31, 2020, the commission received 166 complaints containing 186 allegations. (Some complaints contain allegations of more than one offence.) As of the publication of the statistics, eleven of the allegations had been substantiated, while the rest were either unfounded, withdrawn, did not fit the criteria for investigation by the Public Complaints Commission or were dealt with informally. Thirteen of the allegations were still under investigation.

Regina and Saskatoon are the two largest cities in Saskatchewan, with populations of approximately 230,000 and 260,000 respectively. During that year there were two substantiated complaints in Regina and five in Saskatoon.[14] Based on numbers provided on their websites, Regina responds to approximately 75,000 calls in a year and Saskatoon responds to approximately 104,000. The number of police and civilian interactions is difficult to estimate, since most of these calls for service involve more than one police officer and/or more than one member of the public. Between these two cities one could estimate that there were at least 400,000 police officer interactions with about 400,000 people in the course of the year. Out of all those interactions, there were seven substantiated complaints.

In Ontario, the Durham Regional Police Service (DRPS) serves a population of approximately 705,000 people. Based on the numbers provided on their website, the DRPS probably had about 250,000 interactions between police officers and members of the public during the year 2020. The Independent Police Review Director, whose office handles complaints against police in Ontario, received 148 complaints related to the DRPS during that time. As of the publication of the 2020 DRPS annual report, one of those complaints was substantiated and one was still under investigation.[15]

---

14 Public Complaints Commission, "Annual Report for 2019-20," Saskatchewan, 2020, https://publications.saskatchewan.ca/#/products/107079.

15 Durham Regional Police, "2020 Annual Report," DRPS, 2021, https://www.drps.ca/media/35dbvstu/2020_annual_report.pdf.

There are several reasons why there is such a large difference between substantiated and unsubstantiated complaints. Many complaints are made while a person is upset and, upon further reflection, they withdraw their complaint. Some complaints are completely frivolous or made in order to harass an officer. These sorts of complaints are filtered out by the oversight bodies. There are also many complaints that can be dealt with through an informal channel, often by having the police officer explain directly to a complainant why they did what they did. Most people will be satisfied if they simply listen as a police officer explains why they took a certain action.

You should never let anyone use statistics to trick you. Feel free to do your own research into the number of complaints that are made against your local police agency. What the numbers should say is that there is an enormous amount of policing that happens in your city that is done well and with a high degree of excellence. The slip-ups, the mistakes, and the outright wrongs are the exceptions to the rule.

I want to shift this line of thought to consider another profession. We have all heard anecdotal stories from people who have been sent home from the hospital without a clear answer to their problem, only to return later because the problem persisted. Consider the workload of an emergency room physician. She is working long shifts at all hours of the day and night. She interacts with hundreds of people in a week and many thousands of people each year. Her job is complicated and her decisions can affect lives profoundly. She does not always know the right answer because medical conditions are not always simple, people cannot always clearly explain their pain, and test results are not always conclusive. What room for error do you allow a doctor working under those conditions? Do you concede that even a good doctor might have a five percent error rate? A ten percent error rate? A fifteen percent error rate? What error rate would you allow a police officer? Can she be wrong ten percent of the time?

But What About that Time When ...
I wholeheartedly believe that police do a great job nearly all the time. I strive every day to do my job well and I see that same effort from the other members of my police department. But, yes, sometimes we mess up. One of the themes I hope to convey through this book is that we are human. Some of us have fallen and a few have fallen hard. I am not trying to defend those who have made conscious decisions to break the law or who have tried to hide an error. What I hope to demonstrate is that these things are rarer than you might think; they are the exception, not the rule.

Like any other job, some accidents or mistakes are of little or no consequence. If I am seizing a car and I fill out some paperwork wrong then the car may get towed to the wrong compound. This sort of mistake can be fixed easily. If I fill out the right paperwork, I can have the car towed to the proper compound.

There are other mistakes that are of more consequence but can still be fixed. I can provide you an example from my own career. Years ago I investigated a file in which someone purposely came to police with a false allegation against another person. I acted on the information that was provided, leading me to arrest someone who did nothing wrong. I am happy to say that before I laid charges I listened to her side of the story and discovered tangible evidence that someone had intentionally framed her. She was released without further trouble and given a ride back to her home. I may have scared that woman a little but she was gracious and understood that someone had lied to me and gone as far as to fabricate evidence. She participated willingly in the ensuing investigation until I was able to arrest and charge the person who had used me to try to hurt her.

Of course, there are other mistakes that police officers make that are of much more interest than a slip-up in paperwork. There are different reasons why these things happen and each incident has its own set of circumstances. However, I would like to offer a few words that can serve as general principles.

Sometimes police officers get into trouble because of something they do while they are not at work. Some have been charged with crimes such as impaired driving or domestic assault—two problems that cross all social and economic lines. It is likely that you know someone who has been charged with one of these crimes. You just may not know about it because when these things happen to business owners, yoga instructors, or nurses they do not make the news. And why should they? These things happen every day in my city. They are only newsworthy if they involve someone like a police officer (or perhaps a mayor). And why is this newsworthy? We expect police officers to conduct themselves at a higher level of personal ethics. I think it is appropriate to expect that of police officers. It goes back to the issue of public trust. We are leaders and decision makers for our communities, so we must act like it.

Sometimes police officers get into trouble for things they do at work. One reason a police officer might get into trouble is that he does something that appears to be unprofessional. This sort of thing is hardly newsworthy and might, if confirmed by investigation, result in formal discipline under the laws that govern policing in that province.

In addition, though it happens infrequently, there are times when police officers are charged with a criminal offence for something they did at work. The vast majority of these cases will be in relation to excessive use of force. In Chapter 4, we discussed the use of force and how sections 25–27 of the Criminal Code apply to police officers. When these charges are laid it is often because of something that happened at a call during which force was used and someone later complained that the force was excessive.

If this happens the police officer ends up in the other seat in the judicial proceedings. Just like any other person accused of a crime, he is entitled to a defence and is supposed to be presumed innocent until proven guilty. I have seen some of my own coworkers go through this process and the conclusions are varied. Sometimes they are found guilty but often they are acquitted. I look at it like this: If those officers had been electricians or financial consultants they would not have been involved in many fights at their place of work. The nature of policing is such that we insert ourselves into situations where physical alterca-tions are happening or are likely to happen. The nature of policing is such that we have to walk the line every day between too much force and not enough force. The difference can be of life and death significance, for our-selves, for the person with whom we are dealing, for our fellow officers, and for members of the public. Walking this fine line every day has caused some police officers to say, "I would rather be judged by twelve than carried by six." That is to say, when it comes to violent or potentially violent situations, it is safer to err on the side of caution.

Corruption?

Even in the cases where a police officer is charged and found guilty of excessive force, it does not mean he is a corrupt officer. It may mean that he overreacted or made an error in judgement. In most instances, this happens in the course of an otherwise blemish-free career. The term "corruption" indicates a conscious decision to act contrary to the law. When I was new to policing, even some members of my own family wondered how rampant corruption was among police. I was even asked directly about it. But after ten plus years on the job I can say the same thing I said then: There is not a single coworker that I think of as corrupt. There is no one I want to avoid at a call because I am afraid he will break the law. There is no one who takes money at a drug bust or accepts bribes at a traffic stop. This is because there is really no motivation to do so when the consequences are so high. Police officers in Canada get paid fairly. We have jobs with opportunity for personal growth, training, education, lateral movement, and promotion. We have health benefits and we have pensions waiting for us in the future. Every response I hear from officers to an allegation of corruption refers to these facts. The conclusion is always the same: It is not worth my job to do something so stupid.

That being said, it cannot be denied that some individual police officers have broken the law. Some have stolen things that should have been entered as evidence. Some have lied about their actions. But it must be made clear that this is the exception to the rule. And when these incidents come to light, the officers are held accountable and are likely to be fired.

I have one last comment to make on this topic. Even if there are a few bad police officers among us, even if some have overreacted or some have been unprofessional or some have gotten into trouble, those actions do not define all of us. No group likes to be compared to its worst manifestation and we are no exception. It would be unfair to say that all people who call themselves Muslims want to wage war against the Western way of life. It would be unfair to say that all priests in the Catholic Church are preying on choir boys. Likewise, it would be unfair to say that all police officers are bad because a few have made big mistakes or even fewer have done something wrong on purpose. If you thought about it, you might be able to name more stereotypes that are unfair. There are likely stereotypes that you do not appreciate surrounding a group to which you yourself belong.

The Downside to the Change

Earlier I said that the overall change resulting from civilian oversight and the Charter of Rights and Freedoms has been positive. However, I would like to take a moment to address a danger in this change. It is the danger of weakened policing and the absence of consequences.

As the Charter has been interpreted in case law, many restrictions have been placed on police. One of the trends I see is that career criminals know these restrictions as well as the police do and they are able to hide behind them. In fact, the career criminals train their offspring so well that I meet eleven- and twelve-year-olds who know perfectly well whether or not I have the legal authority to arrest them. In addition to this, limitations on searches mean that procedural errors, such as searching a suspect at the wrong time, often result in damning evidence being ignored by the courts. People who flagrantly commit crimes are acquitted based on technical or procedural challenges that have nothing to do with whether or not a crime was committed. The courts would rather not set a bad precedent by allowing breaches of the Charter, so they ignore evidence, drop charges, and do not hold people accountable for their crimes.

Additionally, the courts have increasingly moved to lighter sentences, including sentences that can be served in the community. I have found that sentences served in the community do not have a high rate of success. The most commonly laid criminal charges in my career are related to breaching the conditions of release from custody. People instructed not to consume alcohol continue to consume. Those who wear electronic bracelets cut them off and leave home. I once heard of a person who was released from court on the condition that he not contact his ex-girlfriend whom he had been harassing. He stepped out of the court building and phoned her to ask for a ride home. This trend has placed a higher workload on police as they chase down convicted offenders who are allowed back into the community and asked to abide by conditions that they blatantly ignore.

Perhaps the worst part is the effect the Charter has had on victims of crime. Often I meet victims who want to cooperate with an investigation but decline to do so because they are afraid of retribution from the offenders. As police, we need to work within the laws. However, those laws will never allow us to arrest someone simply because a victim knows that if she cooperates with us her abuser will make her suffer for it. We do the best we can for victims within the system that exists, but we know the system is inadequate because of the respect paid to the rights of the offenders.

On top of these things, the police have found themselves spending more and more resources making sure they maintain a positive public image. Never before have police departments been so obsessed with public perception. We create entire working positions focused on our public image, paying employees to maintain social media accounts that portray a shiny surface on which the public may gaze. We make our image all about smiles and hugs, not wanting people to know how smelly our work really is. In some ways this has become a necessary evil; public engagement is expected of nearly any organization. However, it distracts from the mission of keeping our communities safe. I would rather have more people next to me on the frontline than more people making public relations appearances and commenting on social media trends.

Alas, this is the world in which we live. Police have diverted resources that could be used to find your stolen car to remind you that some of us are still out there trying to find your stolen car.

7. PERSONAL LIFE

I am standing at attention waiting for the procession to pass. My dress uniform fits tightly but it is not enough to insulate me from the cold early spring breeze. I wiggle my toes to keep them from getting cold or falling asleep in my parade boots.

Along the street in either direction there are perhaps hundreds more people dressed like me, all standing at attention. Many of them are likely thinking the same things I am thinking.

How could this happen? What did our friend experience in his work, the same work I do, that brought him to this place? What made this life not worth living? Is it too selfish in this moment to wonder whether I could ever reach that same place in my mind where I could consider ending my own life?

The procession reaches me. I watch the hearse, black and ominous, as it slowly approaches the church where we will commemorate the life of a man who was, among many other things, a stupendous police officer.

IT IS IMPOSSIBLE TO PROVIDE a detailed account of what the job does to each individual police officer. Each story is unique and we come from a variety of backgrounds, bringing with us a great variety of tools to deal with stress. Once we begin our careers, our experiences are varied. However, there are some themes that can be identified. And I would like to acknowledge that many of the things I say in this chapter are also true for people in other first-responder roles.

Earlier I explained that from day one police officers are trained to see the world differently. We learn to be wary of danger behind every door and around every corner. We learn to be suspicious of people and question their intentions. That adjustment is the beginning of a change that eventually affects the personality of an officer to some degree. As we join a new group of coworkers we become part of the policing subculture.

Once we are working in the community, our experiences cause us to consider the darkness that resides in humanity. We witness the face of that darkness every day. We see people make selfish decisions. We see people engage in self-destructive behaviours. We see anger, hate, bitterness, revenge, and unspeakable violence. We find that everyone we talk to lies to us in order to get out of being held accountable for their actions. What's more, this is as true of the career criminal as it is of the stay-at-home mom who gets pulled over for speeding on her way to soccer practice. While we are at work, nearly everyone we talk to lies.

Each of us has to find a way to categorize and compartmentalize our experiences. We develop ways to make the world we work in feel like it is a different world than the one we live in when we are at home. As an extension of this process, we begin to categorize the people we meet as well. For a police officer, people get divided up into three groups. There are the police, there are the "normal people," and there are the people we spend the majority of our time dealing with, the small fraction of the population that keeps us up at night.

For new officers it can be a struggle to compartmentalize what they are seeing. They have to find a way to be themselves at home and put on a work persona that can deal with the evil at work. However, over time, they might forget that what they see at work, the alternate dimension, is not a common experience. At least, it does not represent the rest of the city. The officers forget that they used to be delivery truck drivers or electricians who enjoyed friendly and carefree interaction with people. They forget that they used to go into the mall with their families and not think twice about their safety or worry about who might recognize them and see that they had small children.

They start thinking like police on days off. Eventually it becomes the way they think about the world. The world becomes a place where people only look out for themselves, people always lie, and people are always selfish. If anyone does something that seems selfless, there must be ulterior motives. It is hard to return to the real world, the dimension in which they were living before starting this job as a police officer. This is what the job takes from us.

Occasionally they are reminded of the people who live without all the problems they see at work. Once in a while people see them standing on their street and step outside to say thank you. Sometimes they are in the home of a break-and-enter victim and he acknowledges the importance of their work or says that he "could never do it." Sometimes people write a note of thanks and send it to the police station. Unfortunately, when they are surrounded by the darkness all day they easily forget that there are people who are thankful for them. When even the "normal people" lie to them to try to get out of a traffic ticket they start to lump them in with the bad guys.

They begin doing weird things that their families notice. They stare into space thinking about something that happened at work the previous night. They avoid certain places like the shopping mall because of the people they might see there. They insist on sitting in the restaurant seat that gives the best view of the room. (My wife has learned to take the other seat because she knows that I want to have my back to the wall so no one can come up behind me in a public place.)

Some start withdrawing from old friends who are outside police circles. Some spend time with coworkers on days off and interact very little with people outside the police world. This makes them forget the rest of the world. If the two groups of people they spend time with are police officers and the people they meet on the job, they forget that those groups only represent a fraction of the population. They may believe there are only two categories of people: police officers and people who hate police officers. The things they read in the news and on social media do nothing to convince them otherwise. That topic has already been discussed, but this is another one of the effects the media can have on the psyche of the police officer.

Police officers typically follow a path that leads to cynicism and a jaded outlook. If that is not bad enough, they find reasons to be cynical about how their own departments are run. There are politics in every workplace and theirs is no exception. Bizarre promotional processes, poor communication, and inconsistency in top-level decision making are points of contention in practically every department.

Shift Work and Sleep

Most police officers start their careers in a shift-work rotation. These come in many forms, usually with ten-, eleven-, or twelve-hour working shifts. The working days are usually lumped into blocks of four, five, or six days, with blocks of three to five days off. There may be four different types of shifts (with start times in the early morning, midday, afternoon, and evening) or there may be only two (day shift and night shift). Some, such as RCMP members in small detachments, are on call because there are only a few members who serve the community and they may be needed at any time.

Most of us did not live a shift-work schedule before we started this job, so this can be a major adjustment. There are some people who can sleep well during the day and there are some who struggle with it. Either way it begins to affect a person; the body suffers when it stays up all night on a regular basis. It can be a struggle to exercise or eat healthy meals because the schedule throws off any routine that one tries to establish.

Over time many officers find they have difficulty adjusting after their night shifts are over. After several years of shift work, their entire first day off may be spent resting. This can even stretch into the second day off, which leaves little time for daily routines and activities before one goes back to work. This affects an officer's health and family life.

Family

There are many ways a career in policing affects family life. In fact, policing is a way of life for the families as much as it is for the police officer. Spouses and children also go through the ebb and flow of the shift-work schedule. There are several days at a time where mom or dad is gone all day or sleeping during the afternoon.

Many policing families experience divorce. A police officer's personality and her outlook on society can undergo significant changes early in her career. Often there is a new group of friends who spend time together on their days off and the spouse is not part of the group. The feelings of camaraderie among police officers can become a strong bond. In fact, police officers often make the comparison that they function as a family, fighting with one another at times but protecting one another when in danger. Shift work means that the spouse has to carry the load at home and in old social circles as the officer is working the evenings and weekends. In some cases, depression or drinking can become barriers in a relationship. In addition to this, a career in emergency services can occasionally lead to mental health struggles.

Managing Mental Health

Over the years a police officer witnesses countless terrible situations. From broken families to fatal car wrecks, gang violence to family violence, sexual assault to murder, we see it all. We are constantly surrounded by evil, death, sadness, anger, and hopelessness.

Police officers develop a set of tools to help them carry on through these experiences. One technique common to every police officer is known as dark humour. This is not unique to policing. One will find dark humour among the ranks of all first responders, emergency room staff, and social workers. Anyone who dedicates her life to working with people in the alternate dimension develops this sense of humour.

Dark humour is the ability to find jokes in the most terrible of circumstances. In effect, this is an extension of compartmentalization in that it removes all emotion from a situation. This is not intended to dehumanize victims. Rather it is a self-preservation technique, intended to ensure that we ourselves remain human. It is a safe-guard for our emotional well-being and it is best that I do not give examples of this humour; it would make me sound unprofessional. I am sure that lawyers have lawyer humour and kindergarten teachers have kindergarten teacher humour. The rest of us may not find it very funny but the people who share those experiences appreciate it. If you could get inside my head I do not expect you would appreciate the sense of humour you'd find there.

Though officers may be equipped with mental health strategies, there are many who are affected by what they see to the point where their mental well-being is in jeopardy. Some see a counsellor or psychiatrist on a regular basis. Some are diagnosed with depression or post-traumatic stress disorder. Some are placed in other work capacities, temporarily or permanently, for the sake of their well-being. I have seen all these things happen to friends of mine.

Post-Traumatic Stress

Some people are deeply damaged by their experiences. Post-Traumatic Stress Disorder (PTSD) is a common diagnosis in police officers. The symptoms of PTSD vary from person to person. Generally speaking, it can cause flashbacks, nightmares, uncontrollable thoughts, or hallucinations. It may be that a person relives an event every time he drives down a particular street.

The experiences that I am talking about are often referred to as critical incidents. Critical incidents, thankfully, tend to happen less frequently. These are not fender benders and neighbour disputes. The following are things that would be considered critical incidents:

- A gruesome murder scene or car accident, perhaps with multiple victims
- Being present when someone dies
- The death of a child
- Horrific abuse of children
- A hostage situation
- An officer's life being in imminent danger
- An officer-involved shooting

- The death of a fellow police officer

Besides these significant experiences, it is possible that an accumulation of events, big and small, can lead to PTSD. An injury of this sort is difficult to identify because the officer cannot point to any one event that has affected her. Perhaps she has worked for a decade with child victims. Perhaps she is a forensics officer who has seen too many murder victims. The change in behaviour can develop slowly and it may be a long time before the officer realizes something is wrong. Perhaps she never identifies the problem so she and her family live in misery for years.

The good news is that the culture is changing, albeit slowly. Issues surrounding mental health are receiving attention and the stigma is being broken down within the police culture as well. Police officers of the previous generation were told to suck it up and keep working. While that may still be the case in some organizations, many have developed policies that recognize mental health concerns and make provisions to help employees who are struggling. I am happy to say that there have been success stories. People have regained their equilibrium after being knocked off their feet by PTSD. But for anyone who has been affected in this way it will mean a lifetime of working through it.

Suicide

While many of those who suffer an emotional injury are able to carry on, this is not true for all. Some, even people I have worked with myself, have been hurt to the point that they will never return to duty. Their lives have been forever changed by things they have seen in their work.

Even worse, some will come to the point that they take their own lives because they believe they cannot continue carrying the burden. This is also true of people in the other branches of emergency services.

I have personally known more than one person who worked in emergency services and ended their own life. It is an unspeakable tragedy that affects families, friends, and coworkers. In a job that can be dangerous, where we train hard to mitigate that danger, the unseen dangers of depression and PTSD lurk in the shadows and take some by surprise. I view suicide as another way that this job has killed many police officers, alongside car accidents, stabbings, and gunfire.

Why I Stay

There are plenty reasons why we should find a career outside of policing. We stay awake all night. We work long shifts. We put ourselves in dangerous situations. We take abuse from both the people we protect and the people we protect them from. We are slandered in the media. We walk a sometimes wobbly line on the spectrum between good and poor mental health. We risk contracting communicable diseases and taking them home to our families. We are disappointed by decisions made by our own management teams.

Yet, with few exceptions, we remain in this line of work for many years. So why is that?

For most police officers the job becomes a significant part of their identity. We think of ourselves as police officers, not as people who work in a police station. A big part of this is related to the fact that we have undergone a shift in personality for this job. We were trained to view the world in a certain way and it is hard to imagine setting that aside.

Perhaps it would be best if I answer this question for myself. I love that every day I go to work I learn something new. Because we deal with people, and people are creative, there will always be a new twist on the things they do. The moment I think I have seen it all someone reminds me that I have not.

I love the camaraderie that exists between myself and my coworkers. We are a team, playing a vital role and dangerous game. I have made good friends and enjoyed working side by side with them, doing a job we know is important. We have laughed together and cried together, though we try not to let you see us doing either.

But the biggest factor is knowing that I am playing a crucial role in society. There are some concrete ways that we, as police officers, see this. When we remove a child abuser from the home and put him in jail, we know we have done something meaningful for that child and her family. When we send a murderer to jail, we are providing a certain degree of closure to a grieving family.

On a rare occasion, we witness a change in a person's life for the better. Over the course of time, many of the badly behaving people we deal with grow up and become mature adults and become a better influence to those around them. Once in a while, one of those people may bump into a police officer and say, "Remember me? I got my life together a while back and I'm doing really well now."

I can pass on one such story that I witnessed. I was part of a large response to a domestic attempted murder in which a young man tried to kill a member of his own family. His life had been on the decline with addiction and the resulting mental health struggles were taking over his decisions. After this eye-opening incident he was given the chance to participate in drug rehabilitation and, to his credit, he participated meaningfully. When his day in court drew near it was apparent to all—family, lawyers, judge, and police officers—that his life truly was on track. He was on a completely different trajectory than he was the day he did something horrible to his loved one. A deal was worked out in which his sentence was to be served in the community, with minor restrictions placed on his freedom. I wholeheartedly agreed with the court that this man should not face time in custody, though his actions were reprehensible. Jail would only have served to hinder his recovery and progress.

However, in policing, there are many things that cannot be measured. We do not know whether the drunk driver we stopped would have killed someone in a car wreck later that night. We do not know how many more people the murderer would have killed if he was not sent to jail for several years. The longer I do this job the more convinced I am that our real successes are in the things we cannot quantify.

I see the things that go on in my city day after day, night after night. I see the kids growing up with no love or reinforcement at home. I see the hopelessness of broken neighbourhoods. I see the dangers that people invite into their lives in the forms of gangs, drugs, and parties. I see the danger that some people pose to the safety of our city. I meet people who do not care if their actions hurt others. I see the wake of destruction they leave in the lives around them. I see how addiction tears lives apart and makes people do things that are hard to imagine or describe.

Nonetheless, though these realities exist, I am convinced that the work that I do allows the people of my city to go about their days without fear. I know of many incidents in which the outcome would be much worse if police did not intervene. Our work truly does provide people with a degree of safety and peace of mind that is not known in many other parts of the world. When people say things about us that we know are untrue, we can hold on to these things. We know that our presence makes the difference between relative peace and complete social chaos. It is an honour to hold that line. For those of us who keep that perspective, our job satisfaction remains high, even during the difficult days. My hope for other police officers is that they keep that perspective.

8. CURRENT SOCIAL ISSUES

I THOUGHT THE WORLD HAD enough problems by the time the year 2019 ended. We had already found plenty reasons to be politically polarized when a new virus, COVID-19, gave us conspiracy theories, anti-maskers, mask-shaming, and the licking of handrails and toilet seats by those who thought their point was worth making in style.

As if that were not enough, in May 2020 the political atmosphere in the United States, already on edge, reacted to a video out of Minneapolis like a powder keg to a match. In the day of social media, millions of people were exposed almost simultaneously to video footage of the death of George Floyd at the hands of a Derek Chauvin, a police officer. The fact that Floyd was a black man and Chauvin was white made a bad situation much worse.

It is important to mention that I have never heard one police officer argue that Chauvin's tactics were correct, his actions justified, or his decision making appropriate. There are clear problems with what happened on that day in May 2020. I cannot explain why Chauvin did what he did. It was wrong, and it went against everything I have been taught about controlling a suspect from day one of my training. We learn to control people, then ensure their safety. Chauvin did one of those things but not the other.

In the wake of that incident I saw a lot of ridiculous things being said about police officers in general, as though Chauvin somehow became a poster boy for the entire profession. I heard the following story from the wife of a police officer about an interaction she had in the weeks following Floyd's death. A friend of hers joined the mob in posting vile things online directed toward police officers. These things were hurtful because they took aim directly at her husband and his chosen profession. Eventually she had the chance to ask her friend about the comments she had made online. She did not understand why her friend would say those things if she knew her husband and the kind of person he was.

She was shocked to hear her friend respond, "Yeah, but your husband is the exception."

I am not certain how long she remained in stunned silence before she responded, "No. Chauvin is the exception. People like my husband are the norm."

If you have heard nothing in my writing that hits home, please hear this. Any misuse of power, any abuse of citizens, any criminal or reprehensible action on the part of a police officer is the exception, not the rule.

During the summer of 2020 I watched as several people connected to my wife on social media also said things that were painful to read. It was at least a year later that my wife turned to me and said, "You know what, during that entire time, not one person ever asked me whether or not the things they were repeating and reposting online were true. Did anyone ask you?" I thought about it for a minute but I could not remember anyone asking me if my experience was in line with the things they were saying about policing.

Meanwhile, things quickly got out of control in the United States. While some protestors burned police stations down others started saying that the solution to the perceived problem was to have less policing. At the same time many people took the opportunity to riot and destroy property. Somewhat ironically, quite a few people, both black and white, were killed during this time of violence.[16] All this was done, ostensibly, to express the fact that black people should not be killed by police officers.

Some of the insights that come from a couple decades of working with people helped me gain a perspective on this. All people are selfish. All people habitually think of themselves before others. But there is a segment of the population who, given the smallest opportunity, will take what they want from others, with no regard for the concerns, safety, or lives of others. There is a segment of the population who are so disconnected from society that

---

16 Jemima McEvoy, "14 Days of Protests, 19 Dead," Forbes, June 8, 2020, https://forbes.com/sites/ jemimamcevoy/2020/06/08/14-days-of-protests-19- dead/?sh=7ba859bc4de4.

causing another death does not concern them in the least. They do not know empathy. By the actions of these people, the image of the entire movement was tarnished. It was difficult to distinguish between people with legitimate concern and people who only wanted to take and destroy.

This is unfortunate because the truth is that there are some in the United States who really have experienced unfair treatment at the hands of the police. But the problems in the United States do not start with the police. Likewise, changing the way policing is done will not fix the root of those problems. Please understand that reducing the quality or quantity of policing will only benefit those who riot and kill.

There are many things in the history of the United States that have made greater contributions to its race issues than any good or bad police officer. That country's founders built their wealth on the backs of slaves. That country worships capitalism to the point of associating universal healthcare with communism. That country built rockets to go to the moon while a black man and a white man still had trouble finding a restaurant in which they could eat together. From its foundation, decisions have been made in the United States with the underlying if not explicit intention of dividing the country in terms of race. There are problems in that country that are much closer to the root of the tree on which any statistic regarding white police officers and black civilians is a high branch.

It is well beyond the scope of this work to make any suggestions about fixing the American justice system. That being said, I do not believe I overstep my field of knowledge to say the following: You should not blindly believe statistics; they only tell a very small part of the story and can be used to mislead. You most certainly should not allow someone in the media or a stranger on the internet to lead you blindly toward a conclusion based solely on statistics. The details underlying the statistics are important—if the statistics are even true at all. You should listen to both sides of a debate and do your research before coming to a conclusion about any issue. Research that merely supports your bias is not research at all. False research, biased research, and a total absence of research are major contributors to our current social condition. Everyone is yelling and no one is trying to understand what anyone else is saying.

I can also tell you that the system of policing in the United States is different in significant ways from that in Canada. Additionally, the problems that face the United States as a country do not always have direct counterparts in Canada. Those who say otherwise are not aware of some of the things that I have tried to communicate through this book. Our history of race relations in Canada, while far from ideal, is different from our southern neighbour. The actions taken to work toward solutions in Canada, while far from adequate, are different from those taken in the United States.

I concede that there have been police officers, both in Canada and in the United States, who should not have been police officers. Sometimes, though it is rare, the hiring process fails us. Sometimes, though it is rare, the job changes people for the worse and they need to leave this line of work. However, my next point is also very important. Just because a few have been bad, it does not mean all are bad. Stereotypes of this magnitude hurt people. As I said earlier, no group of people wants to be associated with its worst manifestation. To do this is to live in a state of small-mindedness. So be very careful before you jump on any bandwagons. The exceptional stories, like that of the death of George Floyd, are notable because they are exceptions.

I believe wholeheartedly that the vast majority of police officers in the United States are also good men and women who are doing an impossible job to the best of their ability under impossible circumstances. By and large, they are to be thanked and applauded for their service. But a few examples of bad police officers—and in greater numbers a lot of poorly handled or wrongly perceived incidents— have combined to create a social upheaval beyond anything my generation has seen.

So while many in the United States come to terms with the possibility of a second civil war, my hope is that people in Canada keep a cool head. I hope Canadians make any necessary course corrections without the riots and death that have occurred to the south. In fact, I believe a number of course corrections have already been made. There are several things that separate policing in Canada from policing in the United States.

I have described some of the changes in Canadian policing over the past forty years. We have the Charter of Rights and Freedoms that guarantees certain rights to all people. We have civilian oversight that keeps police working at a level of professionalism not seen in most other countries in the world. We have systems established for members of the public to make complaints so that we can deal with bad behaviour appropriately. We have partnered with healthcare providers to better understand and serve people who live with mental illness.

In addition to these things, on average we pay our police officers better than most communities do in the United States. This may be a bigger factor than some people think. While I believe wholeheartedly that policing is more than a salary, I also believe that it is important to receive a fair salary. You get what you pay for in life and this applies to policing as it does when hiring a plumber or a wedding photographer. While the system of policing in Canada may not be perfect, it is at the top of the list worldwide when it comes to ensuring fair and professional law enforcement.

Defund, But to What End?

In the wake of the death of George Floyd it was common to hear a new slogan: "Defund the Police!" I feel the need to address this idea directly, as it has caused a lot of stir.

I believe that the phrase "defund the police" means different things to different people. Some people actually believe the world would be better if there were no police officers. Of course, very few serious thinkers would advocate for such a position. In a world with zero police officers, society would crumble quickly into anarchy and the void would have to be filled, most likely by the military. The military trains for combat and survival using bombs, artillery, and small arms. They have no training in de-escalating a domestic argument or talking down a suicidal person. I do not believe this is what most people are asking for so I will not belabour the point.

Some people would like a world with fewer police officers. I am confident that if we made a significant reduction in the number of police officers a few things would quickly happen in most cities of a significant size. All the resources would have to be put to frontline police work. This would leave all the other positions vacant, which would leave investigative sections empty. This means that we would still have the same amount of street-level interactions with police—the work that accounts for almost all violent encounters between police and citizens—but other crucial behind-the-scenes work would be left undone.

There is much important work we would have to abandon. We would not focus on major investigations that target the people bringing drugs into our cities. We would not be able to investigate homicides with as much fervour as we currently do. The same goes for investigations into sexual assaults, violent robberies, or residential break-and-enters. We would not have the resources to properly investigate sexual crimes against children or those who collect and share child pornography. We would not have the resources to keep tabs on those people who have committed such crimes in the past and are now living freely in our communities again. I am certain that no one really wants to see this sort of reduction in policing either.

Defund the SWAT Team

In Chapter 5, I suggested that you should read news articles carefully. I will give the same advice in reference to articles that support the idea of defunding the police.

A common thread among the relevant writings seems to be that the "militarization" of the police has made them too violent. People find police unapproachable because they look like soldiers. They suggest that funding for things like better firearms, tear gas, and SWAT equipment should be the first to be pulled. One article suggests the following:

> If SWAT team deployments were limited to only those situations requiring their equipment and skills, such as hostage-takings and terror threats, there would perhaps be less cause for concern. But similar to previous research conducted in the [United States], we have found this isn't the reality of Canadian SWAT teams. Instead, routine policing represented the majority of SWAT team use.
>
> SWAT teams are increasingly being used by public police for routine activities such as executing warrants, traffic enforcement, community policing, and responding to mental health crises and domestic disturbances.[17]

The wording above is misleading to the highest degree. I have dealt with hundreds of domestic disputes throughout my career thus far. However, I can tell you that I have not asked the SWAT team to help me with any of

---

17 Kevin Walby and Brendan Roziere, "Rise of the SWAT Team: Routine Police Work in Canada is Now Militarized," The Conversation, January 24, 2018, https://theconversation.com/rise-of-the-swat-team-routine-police-work-in-canada-is-now-militarized-90073.

them. That being said, there are domestic situations that do require a more tactical approach. That is because the "domestic dispute" is, in fact, also a hostage situation involving weapons. And I would definitely ask the SWAT team to help me with that.

Just because an event was related to a domestic situation, a traffic stop, or a mental health crisis, does not mean it was benign in nature. Also, there is a very important distinction between executing an arrest warrant for a shoplifting suspect and executing a search warrant for a large-scale drug-trafficking investigation. One requires SWAT and one does not. There is no such thing as a routine execution of a drug-trafficking warrant. The potential for harm is great.

Defund the High School Mentors

Another article suggested that we should end the practice of having police officers work in schools to interact with the elementary and high school population in that context. The author stated matter-of-factly, "Police presence [in schools] has been tied to the school-to-prison pipeline. It can negatively affect the experience of students, as schools have incrementally and increasingly taken on prison-like practices at the expense of student learning."[18] There was a link in the article to a paper written by a faculty member of the University of Florida.

The first few paragraphs of the University of Florida article included descriptions of many horrifying events that have reportedly occurred in schools in the United States. These events include an overzealous security guard (not a police officer) escalating an argument over a mess made in the cafeteria to the point that it became an all-out brawl. The brawl resulted in several students being arrested by the actual police, who arrived after the fact. A subsequent section of the article reads:

> [P]olice officers stationed at schools have arrested students for texting, passing gas in class, violating the school dress code, stealing two dollars from a classmate, bringing a cell phone to class, arriving late to school, or telling classmates waiting in the school lunch line that he would "get them" if they ate all of the potatoes.[19]

---

18 Michelle Stewart, "A Better Future: Howe to Defund and Reimagine Policing," The Conversation, June 11, 2020, https://theconversation.com/a-better-future-how-to-defund-and-reimagine-policing-140413?utm_medium=email&utm_campaign=Latest%20from%20The%20Conversation%20for%20June%2012%202020&utm_content=Latest%20from%20The%20Conversation%20for%20June%2012%202020+CID_8ea28b8a0cb021e718ee73a7bcb6bc79&utm_source=campaign_monitor_ca&utm_term=How%20to%20defund%20and%20reimagine%20policing.
19 Jason P. Nance, "Students, Police, and the School-to-Prison Pipeline," UF Law Scholarship Repository, 2016, https://scholarship.law.ufl.edu/cgi/viewcontent.cgi?article=1782&context=facultypub.

I am forced to read between the lines when provided with so little information. Clearly none of the acts listed above are crimes, with the exception, technically speaking, of the theft of two dollars. It does not take a law degree to realize that no teenager should ever be arrested for arriving late to school. I have to imagine that these minor acts of rebellion led to confrontations between the school staff and the students, which escalated to the point where police were called. If the confrontation between the staff and students did not already constitute a criminal act (damage of property or an attack on the teacher), then presumably the confrontation between the student and the police did.

One other option remains. In Canada we have a provision in the law that allows police to arrest an individual to prevent a breach of the peace. This means that if no crime has been committed and there is no other reason to arrest an individual aside from the fact that their behaviour is out of control, they can be arrested until the police are satisfied the problem will not persist. That person is released without charges. It amounts to putting a person in a timeout as though they were a toddler. Perhaps some of these arrests in American high schools fall under a similar category. Of course, those details are not included in the body of the article.

I perused the footnote that followed the above quotation. I found that there were links to news articles about some of these incidents but most pages were no longer available online. The only link I could follow led me to an article about the student who was arrested for "passing gas in class."[20] The short article explained that the student was "intentionally breaking wind" and shutting off computers. He was charged with "disruption of school function and released to his mother." It seems the author did not feel it was necessary to explain the full story in this instance, which makes me question the accuracy of the entirety of that paragraph. The only information provided was that which was necessary to make a point, a point which is not based on the entire truth. The implication in the article is that the student's flatulence accidentally created a distraction in a classroom. The truth seems to be that the student was deliberately disrupting the learning environment and had to be removed for the sake of the other students' continued education.

I must say that I did not disagree with everything suggested in the University of Florida article. Teachers are now asking police to deal many issues that they used to address on their own. But this is not the fault of the police officers, nor is it always the fault of the teachers. Teachers are no longer in a position to dole out discipline in schools. I am not referring to corporal punishment, but rather to the fact that there seems to be little recourse for a teacher who cannot control her students. As I hear from my own elementary-aged children, it sounds like the teachers have considerably less control over the students than they did when I was their age. And if the teachers are accustomed to calling in the police officer assigned to their school to

---

20 Associated Press, "Student Arrested for 'Passing Gas' at Fla. School," NBC News, November 24, 2008, https://www.nbcnews.com/id/wbna27898395.

deal with issues, they will still call the police for help if they need it, drawing resources from the community to deal with school issues. The school system will not suddenly become capable of dealing with issues just because a police officer is slightly less convenient to locate.

There is a school resource-officer program in the city in which I work. I am friends with several of the officers who have worked in that program. They work in both elementary and high schools. They spend the majority of their time in elementary schools giving presentations to students on topics such as walking home safely or saying no to drugs.

According to one of my friends, the majority of the time in high schools is spent dealing with things such as drama induced by social media. A lot of the work is not directly related to criminal activity but, of course, that was part of the reason for putting officers in schools. It is a mentorship program. Many students actually enjoy positive interaction with a uniformed police officer, which shows them that we are just people, like them, but with an awesome job. Quite contrary to the idea of schools becoming like prisons, the officers working in schools provide necessary guidance to the teaching staff and positive interaction with most students. Occasionally they deal with criminal matters in schools, matters that police would have to deal with anyway, even if they were not conveniently working out of the school office.

The Social Worker/Peace Officer
There is one more topic related to the defund movement that I wish to address. I have heard it said many times that

social workers and addiction counsellors could do much of the work done by police officers. We discussed this in a previous chapter but we need to take a second look at this suggestion. Several things would have to happen if we were to pursue this solution.

First, we would have to convince a lot more people to enter careers in social work and addiction counselling because the need is great. We would have to train them to deal with people who are actually high on drugs or in the midst of a violent breakdown in their mental health. We would have to train them in self-defence because it is guaranteed that they will be attacked by some of their clients. Many of the people they encounter in the streets are likely to be armed. In light of this, I would suggest that these social workers and addiction counsellors would need to be armed with handguns and other less lethal weapons in order to preserve their own lives while they are at work.

It would also be important that these counsellors understand the legal ramifications of using those weapons, since they could be charged with murder if they use them inappropriately. Therefore, classes in Canadian law will form a necessary part of their training. And since these social workers and addiction counsellors are now armed, it might be best to distinguish them from those who are not armed and who work in an office. It would be a good idea for them to wear a uniform or drive vehicles that are clearly marked as "armed social worker vehicles." That way people could wave them down and ask for help when there is a person swinging a baseball bat and swearing at children on a sidewalk next to an elementary school.

These vehicles would require barriers between the front seat and back seat that would ensure the social workers' safety while they are transporting clients who are prone to fits of violence.

Of course, many of the people these armed social workers would try to help will be so high on drugs that they cannot be counselled. For this reason, there should be a place they can take people where they can metabolize the drugs and come down off the high so that afterward they can have a meaningful conversation with them. A hallway with several small rooms void of any dangerous materials would have to be constructed for this purpose. By the time all this work is done, we might begin to recognize these new social workers for what they are: police officers.

What We Actually Need

There are many things police officers do that no one on God's green earth would dare to do while unarmed. This includes the things some people claim could be done by social workers. It is true that we spend a lot of time doing the job of social workers and counsellors, but we are armed for a reason. So when I hear people talk about replacing police with social workers I wish it were that easy.

Unbeknownst to them, what people are actually asking for is more funding, rather than less, and not only for police. We need more funding to help people with mental illness. We need more funding to combat homelessness. More funding for addictions programs that might actually work. More funding to train people for productive living as they try to leave a life of addiction. More funding to provide meaningful training to incarcerated people so that when they are released from jail they have a skill set that is useful in the community and provides a sense of purpose. More funding for private and faith-based organizations that are already trying to do these things on a shoestring budget. And yes, we need more funding for police that includes better training, higher pay to hire quality officers, and additional programs that coordinate our efforts with those of the social workers and counsellors. This would require a more efficient use of government funds. Employing fewer police officers would fix exactly zero problems and it would create an unfathomable amount of new ones.

Racism

One thing people are wondering is whether the things they hear in the news are true. Do police target and abuse people, even assault and shoot people, based upon race or some other visible trait? I have already addressed this in part. Among the police officers I know and have worked with, there is absolutely no desire to be involved in a shooting of any sort. And I'd go further to say the same for *every* police officer. That is the honest and simple truth.

Behind this question lie many more issues than this work is designed to address. Is the history of race relations in Canada perfect? Far from it. Does racism exist in our country? Certainly. Do police services have policies in effect that are intended to discriminate based upon race. Absolutely not. Do individual police officers treat people with less respect based upon race? That is never ever my intention and I do not believe it is the intention of any of my coworkers. In fact, sometimes the opposite is true. Some of us have admitted to one another that we ignore certain things like traffic offences simply because we are trying to avoid accusations of racial profiling. This is particularly true for myself during the times when the media is feasting on a bad policing story.

In reality, most of what we do when we are working on the streets is respond to concerns from the people who call police for help. I have seen calls come to our police service from citizens that appear to be motivated by a racial bias. For example, someone called us one day to report a person wandering on their residential street who did not seem to belong there. The dispatchers asked for a description of the person so that the police could locate the right individual. I was dispatched to this call and was immediately suspicious of the caller's motivation. I wondered what it was about the person wandering on the street that made the caller think he did not belong. Was this a tight-knit community on a quiet residential street and he did not recognize the person? Perhaps, but that alone does not make a person suspicious. Was there some behaviour that was strange but the caller did not describe it to the dispatchers? Was the person looking in the neighbours' windows or taking notes as he looked at the houses? The caller gave no concrete reason for his concern so I cannot answer those questions with certainty. However, it may have been that the person had a different skin colour than all the neighbours.

As a police officer, that put me in a difficult position. I had to respond to this call just like I respond to any other calls, no matter what the motivation is behind them. When

I arrived in the neighbourhood I located the "wandering" person, who appeared exactly as he was described. He was a kind and soft-spoken gentleman, about fifty years old, who had emigrated recently from India. His English was very poor but he was able to communicate that he lived in the house in front of which I found him. His son, whose English was much stronger, came out of the house and spoke with me as well. I tried to explain that I was asked to come and check on his father. I'll admit to you that I even mislead them a little, making it sound more like the caller was concerned for the man's well-being and less like he did not want him to walk on the sidewalk near his home. But no matter how I might dress it up, I drove up the street and stopped a man with dark skin who was, up until that moment, enjoying a solitary walk in his own neighbourhood. Of course, I was not the one who singled him out, but I ended up representing the person who called police.

There were two ways the gentleman and his son could have responded. They could have understood my position, thanked me for doing my job, and carried on with their day. Or they could have taken offence. I am thankful that they responded in the former manner and our interaction was very pleasant, much more pleasant than the thoughts I had about the person who called the police in the first place.

Getting back to the issue of the police officers themselves, I want you to understand the way we approach our interactions with the public. This is very important. In policing, the way we treat people is based upon their behaviour. This cannot be overstated because this factor trumps all the other issues. In Canada, a person of any race, religion, or culture should find that if he is polite and respectful toward a police officer he will be treated respectfully in return. It sounds simple, and it really is that simple. At least that is the culture in which I work in my police department. If your experience is demonstrably different from that, you are free to contact your provincial organization that deals with complaints against police.

On the other hand, people who are rude, defiant, unco-operative, or violent toward police will generate a response that may seem harsh or appear unnecessarily violent to people not familiar with policing. This is because police recognize the signs of danger. Police know that if they allow the other person to call the shots, they are not in control of the situation. The reality is that there are some people who know no other language besides that which is rude, defiant, and uncooperative. Some people cannot speak a civil word to a police officer for any amount of prize money. These are the people I described in an earlier chapter; they live in the alternate dimension, by that other code, in which they play that game with authority. We cannot change them, but we must deal with them daily.

While I would rather spend my day interacting with polite and respectful people, it is more often the case that I interact with the rude, defiant, uncooperative, and violent people. For me, it absolutely does not matter what their skin looks like, what sorts of religious symbols they are wearing, or what their personal lives are like. What does matter is whether or not they can speak civilly, listen to instructions, and cooperate. It bears repeating that I have to consider everyone a threat until I am convinced other-wise. There are markers I watch for that indicate danger.

Race is not one of the markers. I watch for a poor attitude, uncooperative behaviour, minute movements in the body and the eyes, subtle motions that indicate the presence of a weapon, or the fact that the person is searching for an escape from the situation. These are the things that concern me.

There are videos you can find online to demonstrate this point. For instance, if a police officer at a traffic stop does not control an uncooperative subject whom he is trying to arrest he can get injured. If that subject is outside and tries to return to his vehicle, it is often to retrieve a weapon. It cannot be allowed to come to that. I can still remember in great detail one of the videos I watched in training. I saw a police officer pull over an old truck and speak with the driver, an older man, while the two stood behind the man's truck. The man ignored the instructions he was given and then began to make fun of the police officer. When the officer failed to take definitive control of the situation, the man walked back to his truck and retrieved a rifle. Then, from the vantage point of the dash camera in the police car, I watched and listened as that man ended the officer's life. I listened to the officer's last gasps for air as his hopes of going home safely that evening were destroyed along with everything else he hoped to get out of this life.

It really is simple. Calm cooperation is the key to a calm interaction with police. Even people who are the most vile—those who murder their entire family or those who sexually abuse children—will find they are treated with respect if they are calm and cooperative with police. But if a person demonstrates that they cannot remain calm and in control of their actions, the police know they must act to take control of that situation immediately. They know this because they have watched the same videos I have watched and many of them have had their own experiences in the real world that drove home the lesson. We all want to go home at the end of the day, not to the hospital, not to the morgue. Home.

Where We Go From Here

Some people do not want to consider a different side of an issue. Many have built their own version of truth by listening only to voices that confirm what they already believe. But I am ever the optimist. Despite the mess I see in the world, I catch myself thinking that if people were provided with a different perspective there could be greater understanding between the current factions in our society. My hope is that this book may help some people gain a perspective on issues that are points of contention. It is with this same optimism that I would like to suggest there is still more we could do to improve communication between the justice system and the public.

In practically every instance that a police officer commits violence on a citizen he or she is legally and morally justified in doing so. However, there is often such uproar among the public that the details of what actually happened and why it happened, if they are available at all, are drowned out by the noise. I would like to see policing agencies, the court system, and the media make it clear why police are justified in using violence, simply to halt the backlash rather than feed a media monster. If real information were to get out to the public faster, perhaps some people would pause before joining a protest (or a riot) based on a misrepresentation of facts.

I would like to ask the media to present fair information to the public when it comes to self-defence or use-of-force encounters. Do the research and present the truth about why police officers are armed with a variety of weapons and when they are authorized to use them. Present the whole truth, instead of partial truths combined with opinions. I acknowledge that I am not a reporter and don't know the details of the job and, for this reason, I humbly ask that you do the same when you talk about my job.

I would encourage you to do your own research. Find out if your local police department provides some sort of educational program so you can understand more about the people who police your own city. Find out if you are able to ride with a police officer for a shift to see what a day or a night is really like for them.

Please consider the fact that our job demands perfection from imperfect people. Believe me when I tell you we are doing our best but it is impossible to be perfect all the time.

Know that police agencies all around Canada are making efforts to work effectively with people from all cultures, religions, and creeds. Immigration has brought new demographics to nearly every city in Canada and has presented new challenges for policing. People have come to this country from places where police are not trustworthy. We have worked to gain their trust and demonstrate that things are different here. All this work is paying off but there is more work to do. That work continues and, as it does, so will the benefits.

We also need buy-in from the members of our communities. We need leaders to stand up to the people who bring violence to their own communities. We need people to know that we are there to help them. Lack of participation in the justice system is still rampant in some communities and this perpetuates violence. We need people to participate as victims and witnesses so that we can hold offenders accountable before the law.

And finally, I want to thank those of you who trust the police to keep your communities safe. We are honoured to play this part and we hope that the loud voices of a tiny minority do not cause your confidence to waver. We are only getting better at our jobs and we ask that you continue to put your confidence in us.

EPILOGUE: A DAY IN THE LIFE OF A PATROL OFFICER

I ARRIVE AT WORK EARLY on a Sunday morning for my twelve-hour shift. I get dressed into my uniform, putting over twenty-five pounds of equipment on my body. It is going to be more than thirty degrees Celsius today and my ballistic vest is not exactly designed to keep me cool. It will be a sweaty day.

I meet with the other members of my team to be briefed by the sergeant on the highlights of what has happened in our city since I was last at work four days ago. Here I learn that one of my coworkers on another shift was exposed to the blood of someone infected with HIV and he has begun a six-month regimen of drugs that usually make people nauseous to the point of vomiting. I also learn that several of the patrol cars are being used for traffic control at a parade so I will be partnered with Kate. Kate is a great person and reliable police officer, but I like my own space to think during the day. This is a small disappointment but one I do not express aloud.

Kate and I walk outside into the already-blazing sun to find our marked patrol car. We check the equipment and make sure there are no weapons lying in the back seat. This is a daily routine because once in a while we find things left behind by a prisoner who rode in the car without a proper search of his person. Satisfied that our car is ready, I place a magazine containing thirty rounds of ammunition into my semi-automatic rifle and lock the rifle in the rack between the front seats. Feeling my body temperature rising, I sit down in the passenger seat. Kate slides into the driver seat and starts the car. I turn up the air-conditioner.

I have been assigned to pick up video footage from a convenience store where a robbery took place last night. Kate and I head toward the store but the radio interrupts our plans.

We are dispatched to a weapon call in a rough part of town. All the dispatcher knows is that someone was attacked with a machete inside a house and there is lots of blood. Several other police cars are also dispatched with us.

We race across town for several minutes and when the tires grind to a halt on the right street I see that several other police cars are already there. There is a girl about twenty years old sitting on the front steps of the house yelling loudly and incoherently. It is the familiar wail of a person who is both very upset and very drunk. Kevin, my coworker, is standing near the girl at the bottom of the front steps, trying to make sense of what she is saying. Kevin tells me that the other three officers are in the house. Because no sense can be made of what the young woman is saying, Kevin does not yet know if the suspect is still inside the house.

Kate and I enter the house. The smell of sweat, blood, and alcohol—a familiar cocktail—greets us as we hit the top step. There is blood dripped and spread all around the living room floor. I think to myself that I will need new boots after this. Kevin's partner, Marcus, is standing next to another young lady about the same age as the one on the front step. She is crying and yelling curse words. Marcus is holding a kitchen towel on her head and it is soaked with blood. Marcus says he is fine but Chris and Claudia are making their way through the house to see if anyone else is there.

Kate and I join Chris and Claudia in the kitchen. Here the smell is a combination of alcohol, garbage, and dirty dishes. I also see a dirty diaper in the pile of other garbage on the floor. There is a narrow staircase going down to the basement. Kate stays at the doorway to protect Marcus in case someone comes up the steps with bad intentions. The rest of us move quickly to the stairs that lead to the second storey. We mount the steps and then move room to room, finding no one but a three-year-old girl and her five-year-old brother watching a horror movie in one of the bedrooms. There is a jar of Cheez Whiz next to the three-year-old and she is eating from the jar with her bare hands.

We go back down to the main floor and rejoin Kate. We descend the steep staircase to the shallow, unfinished basement and find no one there.

Back in the living room, I have time to take note of just how many empty beer cans and rum bottles there are. There must have been a larger party and it did not end well. Like many other Sunday mornings, the party thrown on Saturday night has only recently ended, and only because someone got angry, grabbed a machete off the shelf on the wall, and slammed it into the forehead of the girl who is cursing on the couch.

The ambulance is pulling up, so Marcus and Claudia walk outside with the girl from the couch. They have to help her walk because she is so drunk she will not make it on her own.

I make a phone call to social services to let them know about this incident and the fact that two preschoolers will need a place to stay for the morning. I head back upstairs to find Kate trying to have a conversation with the five-year-old. He is mostly non-verbal and the words he does know are hard to understand. The three-year-old eats another handful of Cheez Whiz. Kate stands up and asks if I have already called social services. I tell her that they are on their way.

While we wait, I open some windows in an attempt to dilute the smell of garbage, sweat, feces, and blood. When the social workers arrive, they let us know that they have an open file with this family. The girl who is on her way to the hospital for stitches is the mother of the two kids. Her newborn baby is already in the care of extended family members. They tell me they will take these two children to join their little brother at the home of the family members.

Marcus and Kevin tell us that they will complete the reports for this incident. No one knows who the suspect is yet as neither girl wants her friend, brother, cousin, whoever he is, to get into trouble.

Kate and I get back into the car. We talk about the prospects for those kids' future while we drive to the police station. After Kate parks, we both wash our boots in the car-wash bay. I walk upstairs to the change room and trade mine for a clean pair. I walk back outside to the parking lot and find Kate already sitting in the driver seat. I ask her if we can try once more to pick up the video from the convenience store.

On our way to the convenience store, Kate tells me that she thinks her boyfriend will propose to her soon. They have been together for six years and, in her opinion, it's about time. I laugh; she does not.

She is about to tell me more when we come across a car accident. Two cars collided while bringing their occupants to church. No one is hurt and one of the passengers is already on the phone with our dispatcher when we arrive. Kate positions our car to block traffic and turns on our emergency lights.

We speak to the drivers of both vehicles and learn that their stories generally agree. One driver tried to make a left turn but there was not enough time and the other car collided with his rear corner. I compose a quick report that will go to the insurance company while Kate writes a ticket and delivers it to the driver who made the left turn. I call for two taxis because neither vehicle will be able to drive without repairs. We wait while the tow truck loads the vehicles and then we open up the street to traffic again.

Once again, we head in the direction of the convenience store. When we arrive, I speak with the clerk and learn that the manager is not in on Sunday so the video is not ready. I tell the clerk I will try to return tomorrow morning.

Kate and I head back to the car. We politely talk about the investigations we should be working on, neither of us saying it would be easier to do so if we did not have to share a car today. We agree to go speak with someone whose vehicle was involved in a hit-and-run last week. Kate was assigned to investigate this incident.

We arrive at the house and the owner of the offending vehicle opens the door. Kate tells the man why we have come to speak with him and he allows us into the house. When Kate explains the incident, the man says he was in the parking lot on the day in question but he did not believe he was in an accident.

We all walk into the garage where the vehicle is parked. There is paint scraped off the front passenger-side corner and a crack in the plastic bumper—typical damage for an accident of this sort. The damage is consistent with the account given to police by a witness and the video footage from a security camera.

Kate writes a ticket because it is illegal to damage another person's vehicle and not leave a note identifying yourself. The man is not happy about it and says he will fight the ticket. Kate explains that it is his right to go to court and he rudely replies that he will see her there. The door slams behind us as we walk down the front steps.

We drive aimlessly for about seven minutes, bemoaning the existence of self-righteous people who think they should not be held accountable for damaging someone's car in a parking lot. There was enough damage that he should have noticed. He just drove away; we are sure of it.

The dispatcher calls our number again. They have someone on the phone screaming hysterically that their baby is not breathing. Kate snaps the lights and sirens on and drives fast enough to scare me a little.

We work together, watching for hazards as we speed toward the address. As we slow down for the red traffic lights I help Kate watch for traffic and when I yell that it is clear she accelerates as fast as the vehicle will allow. As Kate makes the last left turn, the tires screeching along the hot pavement, I release my seatbelt.

This time we arrive first and I am running toward the house before our car comes to a complete stop. Kate is close behind me. The front door is open and I run inside. In the living room I find a seventeen-year-old girl crouched next to the couch crying and screaming unintelligibly. I see a baby lying on the couch. Just as I come alongside the young girl I am relieved to hear the ambulance arriving. Very soon, the EMS members run into the house. They work on the baby at a furious pace while I watch.

Kate tries to talk to the young girl and slowly learns, between sobs and wails, that she is the mother of the baby. She says she and the baby had a nap that morning and when the girl woke up the baby was not moving.

One of the EMS members announces that they will rush the baby to the hospital. Even as he says it, I catch his eye and understand that he does not believe he can help the baby. I follow the EMS member who is carrying the baby out of the house. I see Jim getting out of his police car and I quickly tell him what is happening. Jim will secure the house for further investigation. Kate walks the young mother to our police car to give her a ride to the hospital while I get into the back of the ambulance.

Before we arrive at the hospital the EMS members tell me that they are certain the baby has passed away. Nonetheless, they keep working.

When we arrive, the baby is rushed into an emergency room where a team of doctors and nurses await. I watch in awe, as I do every time, while the team of six healthcare workers move and speak in a rhythm that they have developed over the course of caring for hundreds of trauma patients. Despite their efforts, after six minutes the doctor pronounces time of death as 10:34 a.m. Detaching myself from the horror around me, my next thought is that it seems I have been at work for longer than three and a half hours.

The doctor steps out of the room to inform the young mother that her baby has passed away. I can hear her wailing from down the hall.

I phone my sergeant to let him know what has happened. About ten minutes later he walks into the emergency room where I am still waiting with the small body. My sergeant tells me that the homicide detectives will be coming to take over the investigation. They do so in these cases, not because we assume this is a homicide but because it is a death that requires a thorough investigation.

The homicide detectives arrive about forty minutes later. Kate and I tell them all we have learned so far and then we walk to our car in silence. In the car I deliver a short rant about how people really have to stop sleeping with their newborn children beside them. This is often the cause of a death like this and it happens often enough to rile me.

At the police station we spend about an hour typing reports and now it's time for our lunch break. We do not always get the time to go for lunch so this is welcome news. Kate heads for the gym and I drive home to see my family.

I hug my wife and kids and tell them the day has been busy but good so far. The kids wander off and I start making a sandwich. As I sit down at the table to eat I tell my wife about the baby. She asks me how I'm doing. I say I'm fine and I believe it's true.

As our lunch break ends I drive back to the police station to pick up Kate. I wait for a minute in the parking lot before she walks out of the building and toward the car. No sooner has she sat down in the passenger seat than the dispatcher calls our number. We are sent to a domestic dispute at a house close to where Kate lives.

On the way there I ask if she knows the people involved. She tells me that she knows a few of her neighbours but this house is on the crescent adjacent to hers and she does not know anyone on that street. From time to time we run into people we knew as kids or played sports with in college. Depending on the circumstances, those calls can be a little awkward.

When we arrive we knock on the door and it is answered by a woman who appears to be about forty years old. I see that her left cheek has a red mark on it. I ask the woman to step out onto the front deck to speak with Kate while I go inside. As she steps through the doorway she tells me I can find her "sack-of-crap husband" in the living room.

I find the "sack of crap" sitting on the couch cracking a can of beer. I politely ask him to tell me what happened that afternoon. I listen to a four-minute-long story that is delivered as a tirade. I quickly discern that this is not the first can of beer he has had today. If I believed every word coming from his mouth I would say he is clearly married to one of the worst women in our city. Of course, that is if I believed him. I do not believe much of what he is saying. After four minutes I have to interrupt him. I ask again what happened leading up to the time the police were called. He tells me that after they argued all morning he told his wife he wanted time alone and went to the bedroom. When she followed him into the room he pushed her back out so he could close the door.

Kate steps inside the house and quietly announces to me in code that there is an allegation of an assault. She also gestures to her cheek and I know that the red mark I saw is the result of the so-called push. The word "push" must mean "punch in the face" in this home, as it does in many other homes I have visited. It's all semantics, I suppose.

I tell the man that he is under arrest for assault. He yells at me in that slurry drunken way, "I didn' 'sault no one; she 'sssaulted me." Funny. He did not mention that even once during the four-minute tirade. I am able to slip in behind the man and put handcuffs on him before the yelling turns to something more violent. In order to get him to the police car we have to walk past his wife of twenty years as she waits in the front yard. He unleashes a string of curses in her direction and she responds with words and hand gestures of a similar nature.

In the car, I try to read the man his rights. I ask him whether or not he understands the rights and whether or not he wants to phone a lawyer. I receive only insults and curse words in response. In my notebook I record his exact words, vulgar though they may be. I also write down the time. Six more hours to go today. I am just starting to feel a dull headache coming on. I roll my neck to try to loosen it up. I do not know why I do it; it never works.

As we drive to the police station the man calms down to the point where he is giving us the silent treatment. This is a lot better than when he was talking. During this drive I hear the dispatcher call for several cars. She sends them to a residential neighbourhood where a middle-aged man was walking down the street with a rifle. Just as the call was coming in, the caller saw the male walking between two houses and into a backyard. Practically every available car is sent to the call but, since we have a customer in the back seat, all we can do is listen to the radio as this call progresses.

We arrive at the police station and drive into the parking garage outside the detention block. As we search the husband-of-the-year before placing him in his cell he announces that he would like to call his lawyer. Whenever someone says "my lawyer" it is usually a hint that he has been in trouble before.

After the man calls his lawyer I escort him to his cell. Next, I go to a computer to check his history with the police. It turns out he has been in trouble a couple times. He has been arrested for impaired driving twice and he has assaulted his wife once before (that we know about).

I contact the sergeant who is overseeing the rifle call to see if he needs us. He says he has enough people for the time being but if something changes he will let us know.

The next twenty minutes are spent writing a report regarding the domestic assault. During this time I hear on the radio that the male with the rifle ran out of a backyard and was arrested in the alley. For some reason he left the rifle under the back deck in the yard. When the rifle was retrieved there was a round of ammunition found in the chamber.

The city is now getting quite busy. Over the radio, the dispatcher asks people to finish their calls to attend new ones. A couple people respond that they are finished on the rifle call and can help take the next calls.

My sergeant enters the room as I am finishing my report. He reminds me that I need to finish some work for him so he can complete my annual performance assessment. Then, without waiting for a response he asks, "Are you doing something important? They need you out there."

Kate and I abandon our reports and head out to the car. I radio the dispatcher to let her know that we are at her disposal. Before she can respond I hear the K9 handler, Will, announcing over the radio that he is following a stolen car through a rough part of town. Will says the driver of the car seems to have figured him out and the car is now making quick turns and doubling back. Will backs off a little.

I get into the driver seat and start driving in Will's direction, knowing that he will need help if the driver ditches the car. Sure enough, within a minute Will is back on the radio saying that he has found the car, abandoned in an alley, and he wants to track the driver with his dog, Shark.

I pick up the pace. Over the radio I tell Will that I will come and assist him with the track. While we race into the area where Will is waiting, I hear a couple more people on the radio saying they will leave what they are doing to help.

Forty seconds later we arrive in the alley where Will and Shark are waiting for me. The dogs always know when they are going to go for a run. Shark is pulling at the leash and Will his holding on with both hands. I stop the car, unlock my rifle, and step out of the vehicle. I rack one of the thirty rounds of ammunition from the magazine into the chamber of the rifle. Kate runs around the car and gets into the driver seat. She leaves the alley in a hurry, on her way to help other cars set up a containment perimeter around the area.

Will tells me that Shark wants to track to the west. I follow Will, close enough to protect him if somebody jumps out from behind a fence but not so close that I get in his way. I do not want Shark to take much notice of me. If I get in his way, he may mistake me for the one he is supposed to apprehend. Due to my own lack of self-awareness, he has bitten me once before. It was not a good experience.

Sometimes I wonder why I love this job so much. We run down the alley, cross a street, and enter another alley. It is my job to keep Will safe while he concentrates his efforts on following the lead of the dog. Sweat is running down my back as I run.

Every time I run with Will it hits me. I cannot believe that this is my job. I get paid to run through town with a rifle. Between Will and myself, we are carrying about 250 rounds of ammunition. I am carrying five objects on my belt defined as prohibited weapons in the Criminal Code, not legal for people to carry unless they are doing my job. What a strange line of work.

My thoughts are interrupted by Shark. He has just rounded a corner and as Will and I follow him we see a shirtless male running down the street away from us. He is the only person in sight and Shark is barking furiously. Will yells loudly to the male to stop before he lets go of the leash. The male stops, turns to face us, and shoves his hands into his pockets. Will tells the male to put his hands where he can see them but they remain where they are.

Shark continues to work and tracks directly towards the male. Soon we are tracking over the place where we first saw him running away from us. The male starts yelling back at Will, using words that I hope my kids never learn. I have moved over to Will's right, farther away from him and Shark so that, if necessary, I can take a shot without endangering them.

Will tells the male a second time to take his hands out of his pockets and lay down on the ground. No cooperation, just more profanities directed at Will. Will, Shark, and I come to a stop. I am standing about ten metres away from the suspect and I can see that he is about seventeen years old. I am aiming my rifle at the ground about a metre in front of his feet, ready to be raised and aimed at him if necessary. Will yells louder, competing with the volume of the barking German Shepherd, telling the kid to take his hands out of his pockets very slowly. Finally, the hands come out of the pockets in a fast jerking motion. As they do every muscle in my body tenses. I flinch a little as I anticipate the unthinkable. Thankfully, the hands are empty. I make a mental note that my trigger finger was what flinched when his hands came out of the pockets. Will tells the kid he is under arrest for possession of a stolen vehicle and orders him to lay down on the ground. He complies, slowly, and not without more insults being launched at both Will and me.

Will radios to the cars on the perimeter that the suspect has been found but he is not yet in custody. I hear roaring engines and screeching tires as several police cars abandon their positions and come to our assistance. Neither Will nor I move. My rifle is still aimed at the ground beside the teenager and he is still calling names.

The first cars arrive and I see Tyler and Elliott approach from my right. I tell them I will keep my rifle out while they take custody of the kid. Together we approach the young man, who is still insulting everyone within earshot. I keep guard while Tyler and Elliott put handcuffs on the suspect. Once the handcuffs are secured, I lower my rifle and hang it over my shoulder on its sling. I breathe deeply, waiting for the adrenaline to run its course through my body. Tyler and Elliott search the kid before standing him up and walking him toward their police car. All they find in his pockets is a bag of drugs.

I see Kate pull up in our car. I walk to the car, unload the round of ammunition from the chamber of my rifle, and then secure the rifle in the rack. We have a conversation with our coworkers, dividing the work that needs to be done on this call. Since Tyler and Elliott have the suspect, I tell Will that Kate and I will take him back to his vehicle, then deal with the stolen car.

Will and Shark get into the back seat of our police car. Tongue hanging out, Shark is still breathing hard. He gets flatulent when he is excited. Kate opens all the windows and plugs her nose in a joking gesture that only I see. The car smells a little worse when we arrive in the alley, though neither the canine or the human in the back seat seem to have noticed.

Kate and I call for a tow truck and fill out the necessary papers to document the recovery of the stolen car. Because we did not actually find the driver inside the vehicle, I include a request for a member of the forensics unit to process the vehicle for fingerprints. My hope is that they may confirm what the dog has already told us, that the suspect we apprehended was in the stolen car moments earlier. The tow truck arrives and takes the car away.

By this time there are only three hours left in our shift. I start to think about how nice it will be to get out of my sweaty uniform. The air-conditioner is running at full power in the vehicle and slowly I start to cool off. I ask Kate to get me back to the police station so I can use the bathroom. On our way there she asks about the arrest of the car thief. I tell her about the way the kid put his hands in his pockets, almost taunting or tempting me. She shakes her head and says, "One of these days someone is going to get themselves shot doing something stupid like that." I nod. I know that it could have been today.

After my quick stop at the bathroom, Kate drives the car around the city. We wait to see what will happen next. It only takes six minutes for the dispatcher to call us again. She sends us to check for a person who is looking in garbage bins in the back alley of a residential area.

The caller provided a vague description of the person. For whatever reason the caller believed the person in the alley was up to no good. The communications personnel asked what exactly was suspicious about the person's behaviour but no concrete reason was given.

There is no hurry to a call like this so Kate takes her time, moving with the flow of the late-Sunday-afternoon traffic.

We find no one in the alley behind the caller's home. We drive around the neighbourhood, wandering through other alleys as well, but find no one matching the description provided by the caller. We clear the call.

Less than five minutes later the dispatcher calls us again and sends us to another domestic dispute, this time in an apartment building. The caller can hear the neighbours above her screaming and stomping on the floor. She says the argument has been going on for about an hour.

We hurry to this call and arrive four minutes later. A resident who just happens to be arriving home with her groceries lets us into the building. We find the fourth floor and follow the noise to the correct door. I have to knock loudly to be heard over the shouting that is going on inside the apartment. The door opens wide and a young man in his mid-twenties steps back to let us inside. Gesturing wildly with his arms he says, "Look who finally showed up! I told you someone would call them." He is looking directly into my eyes as he says the words but he is clearly addressing the young woman standing behind him in the living room.

Once again, Kate and I separate the two people and have individual conversations with them. This time we learn that there was no physical altercation between the two and they have merely been arguing over money and how they will deal with issues related to the kids. I ask the young man how we can make certain the fight is over and he says he will gladly catch a taxi to his friend's house to spend the rest of the day there.

We say goodbye to the young woman, leaving her with three young children in the apartment. Kate and I head down the stairs with the young man to wait for the taxi. Standing on the sidewalk, we make awkward small talk for about ten minutes until his taxi arrives. Once the taxi has taken him away I get back into the police car.

Kate and I start driving out of the neighbourhood. She asks if I have any plans for our next set of days off. My wife and I are planning a camping trip with the kids and I start to tell her about it.

Soon we are on a wider street with three lanes moving in each direction separated by a boulevard. The traffic is still quite light, as it is now about dinnertime on a Sunday evening. I notice a small pickup truck roll through a stop sign and turn right, entering the street directly in front of us. I see that the truck is picking up speed quickly and it's soon pulling away from us. This street has a speed limit of sixty kilometres per hour and it is obvious the truck is going quite a bit faster than that. I point at the truck and Kate nods. She starts picking up speed as well and turns on the lights and siren. Soon we are going ninety kilometres per hour and barely gaining on the truck.

The truck brakes hard and makes a right turn onto another residential street. It picks up speed again but this time only makes it up to about forty kilometres per hour.

I radio the dispatcher and announce we are trying to pull over the truck. Just as I do so, it begins slowing down. The truck is still not stopping but it is going slower, then slower. I see the driver drinking water and I point this out to Kate; he is likely swallowing bags of drugs before we can stop him. Slower. Slower. Finally, the truck comes to a stop and I see the reverse lights flash, telling me the driver has placed the gearshift in park.

I get out of the police car quickly and approach the driver side of the truck. Kate stays back for a short time, radioing our location to the dispatcher. When I get to the driver's door I find the window closed. I pull on the door handle and realize it is locked. I speak loudly so the driver can hear me through the glass and I tell him to roll down the window. The window rolls down and the driver starts yelling back at me that he was not speeding. In the short time it takes him to say this I notice that the pupils of his eyes are very small and he is not focusing on my face when he yells at me. I already have a few reasons to suspect that he is high on drugs and I do not want him driving any further.

I reach inside the window and pull up on the lock. I open the door and back up, telling the driver to get out of the truck. His only response is to yell profanities at me. I see him reaching for the gear shift and without thinking I grab his left arm as tightly as I can with both of my hands and pull on it very hard. I knock the driver off balance enough that when I pull a second time he tumbles out of the truck. As he tumbles he wiggles free from my grasp. He catches himself before he falls and stands up near the open driver's door. Now that I see him standing up in front of me I realize that he is a lot larger than I am. I tell him he is being detained because I suspect he is driving while impaired. As I reach for his arm to get control of him he pushes me away again.

Now the whole thing is just a mess. He is yelling at me that he did nothing wrong and I am yelling back, telling him he is under arrest. I try to grab his arm and move to handcuff him but he is able to push me away again. I try one more time, grabbing a handful of clothing to try to pull him down to the ground so I can gain control of him but again he just pushes me away. He is huge and there is no way that I can win a fist fight with him. He would hurt me badly.

I notice that Kate is holding her taser and I back away. I notice that the driver is inching back toward the open door of the truck. Kate yells at him that he needs to get on the ground but he keeps moving toward the driver seat. Kate fires the taser.

Thankfully the day was hot and the driver was only wearing a T-shirt. The prongs make contact and stay in place. The driver drops to the ground. I wait until the taser stops, then jump in quickly and get one handcuff onto the left wrist. The driver is flexing all his muscles but he is not fighting me anymore and after a few seconds I am able to get the handcuff onto the other wrist.

The adrenaline hits me immediately. I put my knee down onto the driver's hip, not necessarily to keep him down, but to keep myself from falling. My leg starts shaking. Kate asks if I'm all right and I ask her the same question. We both say we are fine.

I hear sirens. Kate must have radioed for help but I never noticed her do it. It takes about forty seconds for the next car to arrive. When it pulls up Marcus jumps out and runs over to where I am still kneeling down next to the driver of the truck. Marcus helps me stand the driver up and walk him to his police car.

My sergeant also arrives. I inform him that Kate fired her taser. He takes Kate's taser from her and puts it in his police car.

I look in the truck through the driver's door that's still wide open. I see some small bags of what looks like cocaine in one of the cup holders. In the other cup holder is a thick roll of cash. On the passenger seat I see a scale and some empty plastic bags, signs of drug trafficking. Not only has this guy been using drugs, he has also been selling them. I also know that when people are selling drugs they are usually armed. I look a little closer and find a handgun underneath the driver's seat. Before I start collecting all these items I walk over to where Marcus is still sitting in his car with the driver of the truck. I let him know of a few more charges for which the driver should be arrested. I return to the truck and start collecting the items. When I pick up the handgun I find seven rounds of ammunition in the magazine and one in the chamber.

By the time all the items are collected from the truck, a tow truck has arrived. After the tow truck hauls the small pickup truck away Kate drives us back to the police station. We spend the next hour weighing the drugs and documenting the items I seized. The rest of the paperwork will have to wait until tomorrow morning since we are already an hour past the end of our shift.

Finally, I walk to the change room and take off the sweaty uniform. As I walk out of the police station toward my car I am thankful that I get to go home for a late dinner and what I hope will be a good sleep. I'll be back in less than twelve hours for another day at work.

BIBLIOGRAPHY

Adhopia, Vik and Melanie Glanz. "Pandemic Worsens Canada's Deadly Opioid Overdose Epidemic." CBC News. June 10, 2020. www.cbc.ca/news/health/drug-overdoses-covid19-1.5605563.

American College of Emergency Physicians Excited Delirium Task Force. "White Paper Report on Excited Delirium Syndrome." Academia. September 10, 2009. https://www.academia.edu/1131068/ACEP_Excited_Delirium_White_Paper_Contribution_via_CA_Hall_MD_FRCPC.

Associated Press. "Student Arrested for 'Passing Gas' at Fla. School." NBC News. November 24, 2008. https://www.nbcnews.com/id/wbna27898395.

Canadian Association of Chiefs of Police. "National Use of Force Framework." CACP. November, 2000. https://www.cacp.ca/cacp-use-of-force-advisory-committee.html?asst_id=199.

Durham Regional Police. "2020 Annual Report." DRPS. 2021. https://www.drps.ca/media/35dbvstu/2020_annual_report.pdf.

Dalrymple, Theodore. *Life at the Bottom: The Worldview That Makes the Underclass.* Chicago: Ivan R. Dee, 2001.

Fredericton Police Force. "2021 Annual Report." Fredericton Police Force. 2022. https://www.fredericton. ca/sites/default/files/fredericton-police/fredericton_ police_2022_annual_report_english.pdf.

Government of Canada. "Corrections and Conditional Release Act." Justice Laws Website. November 1, 1992. https://laws-lois.justice.gc.ca/eng/acts/C-44.6/index.html.

Henley, Tara. "Speaking Freely: Why I Resigned From the Canadian Broadcasting Corporation." Substack. January 3, 2022. https://tarahenley.substack.com/p/ speaking-freely?utm_source=%2Fprofile%2F15756028-tara-henley&utm_medium=reader2&s=r.

McEvoy, Jemima. "14 Days of Protests, 19 Dead." Forbes. June 8, 2020. https://forbes.com/sites/ jemimamcevoy/2020/06/08/14-days-of-protests-19-dead/?sh=7ba859bc4de4.

Nance, Jason P. "Students, Police, and the School-to-Prison Pipeline." UF Law Scholarship Repository. 2016. https://scholarship.law.ufl.edu/cgi/viewcontent.cgi?article =1782&context=facultypub.

Public Complaints Commission. "Annual Report for 2019-20." Saskatchewan. 2020. https://publications. saskatchewan.ca/#/products/107079.

Solzhenitzyn, Aleksandr. "A World Split Apart." The Aleksandr Solzhenitsyn Center. June 8, 1978. https://solzhenitsyncenter.org/a-world-split-apart.

Stewart, Michelle. "A Better Future: How to Defund and Reimagine Policing." The Conversation. June 11, 2020. https://theconversation.com/a-better-future-how-to-defund-and-reimagine-policing-140413?utm_medium=email&utm_campaign=Latest%20from%20The%20Conversation%20for%20June%2012%202020&utm_content=Latest%20from%20The%20Conversation%20for%20June%2012%202020+CID_8ea28b8a0cb021e718ee73a7bcb6bc79&utm_source=campaign_monitor_ca&utm_term=How%20to%20defund%20and%20reimagine%20policing.

Supreme Court of Canada. "R v. Fearon." Supreme Court Judgements. December 11, 2014. scc-csc.lexum.com/scc-csc/scc-csc/en/item/ 14502/index.do.

Supreme Court of Canada. "R v. Lloyd." Supreme Court Judgements. April 15, 2016. scc-csc.lexum.com/scc-csc/scc-csc/en/item/15859/index.do.

Von Kliem, J.D. "The 21-Foot 'Rule' is Back in the News!" Force Science. September 12, 2019. https://www.forcescience.com/2019/09/the-21-foot-rule-is-back-in-the-news.

Walby, Kevin and Brendan Roziere. "Rise of the
SWAT Team: Routine Police Work in Canada is Now
Militarized." The Conversation. January 24, 2018. https://
theconversation.com/rise-of-the-swat-team-routine-
police-work-in-canada-is-now-militarized-90073.

Winnipeg Police Service. "2021 Statistical Report."
Winnipeg Police Service. 2022. https://winnipeg.ca/
police/AnnualReports/2021/AnnualReport.pdf.

www.ingramcontent.com/pod-product-compliance
Lightning Source LLC
Chambersburg PA
CBHW020316290526
45785CB00007B/2816